Books by Don

My Grandchildren's America Will it Still be the Land of the Free and the Home of the Brave

Goodbye Constitution Freedom America

The Road to Tyranny Individualism to Collectivism

Two Visions of America

Setting Brushfires of Freedom

Books available:

www.mygrandchildrensamerica.com

www.amazon.com

Setting

Brushfires

Of

Freedom

Setting

Brushfires

Of

Freedom

Don Jans

ISBN   978-0-578-68193-1

COPYWRIGHT PENDING   2020

SMEA PUBLISHING

PREFACE

In the 1760's, 1770's, and 1780's, the people living in the American colonies suffered much to win their freedom and independence from King George and Parliament, who the American patriots viewed as a tyrannical government. The predominant sentiment in the earlier years seemed to be a view that would have the people finding a way they could co-exist with their motherland, Britain. One of the patriots that stood apart from the rest was Samuel Adams, who never considered co-existence. Samuel Adams always had as his ultimate goal, complete separation, and independence of the colonies from what he viewed as the tyrannical rule of King George and Parliament.

In "Setting Brushfires of Freedom" I have used Samuel Adams as the prime example of how eventually the American colonies did declare independence from Britain and then went on, against very great odds, to win their freedom. Samuel Adams was a master writer and used the published word skillfully. He understood when to attack and when to cajole. He understood who he was, and he understood who opposed him and why they opposed him.

The nation that Samuel Adams helped to establish was an incredibly unique nation. The United States was the first nation to be founded on the principle that all people have been endowed by the Creator with inalienable rights. The only role the government has in this scenario is to protect those rights for the people. The United States was also founded as a republic. Our founders purposefully did not establish the United States as a democracy. They had many reasons for this, but predominantly they believed that rights should be for all people, both the majority and the minority, and they knew that democracy always became despotic.

What we know in the 21st century is that these principles, natural rights, and a republic, are not understood, and even worse are not valued. Many people in the United States today are advocating for exactly the opposite of what the founders established, and that is that all rights should be under the total purview of the government and our republic should be abandoned and replaced with a democracy.

I do explain the reasons why this should not happen, if in fact the people of the United States wish to remain free and independent and not again come under the tyranny of government.

There is a movement within the United States to change us to a collectivist nation, a nation where government dictates how all are to live and even how all are to think. The term collectivist is an all-encompassing word for Marxism, communism, socialism, and the progressive movement. Over the years, how a nation is to be transformed into a collectivist nation has been stated many times in different ways.

The mandatory principles that must be infused into a society for a transformation to occur have been consistent in each of the of the methods. That an indoctrination system must be established, and the basic unit of the family must be destroyed, along with others, is always a part of the transformation to the collectivist system. For my purposes, I have used as standards for implementing the transformation, The Communist Manifesto, Lenin's

Decalogue, and the 45 points entered into the United States Congressional Record in 1963.

Just as I outline the events that led to the signing of the Declaration of Independence and how Samuel Adams was involved, and how he used them to continue the movement toward independence, I have also shown how these different "road maps" for transformation are being implemented and followed.

I believe it is safe to say most Americans are not aware of how determined Samuel Adams was in his resolve that the colonies should be a free and independent people. I believe it would be safe to say that most Americans have forgotten or were not taught the different events that led to the 1st Continental Congress and the eventual drafting and signing of the Declaration of Independence.

I believe it is safe to say most Americans do not understand why our founding was so unique in that we are a nation whose founding was based on the concept of Natural Rights. I believe it is safe to say most Americans are not aware of the differences between a democracy and a republic and why our founders were so adamant about our nation being a republic.

I believe it is safe to say that most Americans are not aware that prominent people in the United States have called for the transformation of our country. It is the same transformation that was outlined in the sources I mentioned above; The Communist Manifesto, Lenin's Decalogue, and the 45 points entered into the Congressional record.

If Freedom Loving Americans are determined to thwart this transformation and keep the United States a free and independent nation where the people are not under the tyranny of government, then they must move forward with the same resolve of Samuel Adams. That means they must become a part of the minority to which Adams refers when he told us brushfires of freedom must be set.

There are things that a Freedom Loving American must do prior to setting those brushfires of freedom. The Freedom Loving American must understand who they are, what they believe, and why they believe it. They must also understand who are these people that wish to transform the

United States, what do they believe, and why do they believe it.

For some Freedom Loving Americans, the first part is simply a refresher course, while for others it might be learning things they have never known before. I do have reason to believe that for all Freedom Loving Americans, learning who these people are that wish to transform the United States is well known, but not the part about what they believe and why they believe it. This is critical. Abraham Lincoln understood Stephen Douglas, who he was, what he believed, and why he believed it as well as did Stephen Douglas. You must do the same concerning those who wish to transform the United States.

Once the Freedom Loving American has learned this information, and it is not nearly as daunting as it sounds, they must understand how to set brushfires of freedom. It is not successfully done by telling the other person a thing or two. It is not successfully done by arguing or by debating. It is best accomplished by listening and asking questions that in turn will cause the other person to begin to question why they believe what they believe and that perhaps there is a better way.

This is discussed, along with different examples. There is no better person than you and no better time than now to begin this process. Ronald Reagan famously said, "If not us, who? If not now, when?"

1981 Reagan speech:

"All of us came here because we knew the country couldn't go on the way it was going. So, it falls to all of us to act. We have to ask ourselves, if we do nothing, where does all of this end. Can anyone here say that if we cannot do it, someone down the road can do it, and if no one does it, what happens to the country? All of us know the economy would face an eventual collapse. I know it's a hell of a challenge, but ask yourselves if not us, who, if not now, when?"

I began to consider this book as much as two years ago. During the Question and Answer portion of my talks, I was often asked, "so what do we do." It became apparent to me that this was a very genuine question. I begin to reverse (This is a method you will learn about in this book. It is an amazingly effective method if you are interested in learning and not telling.) that question and learned that a book of this nature is truly needed. As you read it, I believe you will agree with me.

As I said, I learned much when reversing that question, so a sincere thank you to all of you wonderful patriotic Americans, who so patiently explained to me why you asked that question. I owe you gratitude for not just the information you gave me, but also for planting the seed that led to the initial outline and finally the writing and printing of "Setting Brushfires of Freedom."

I also owe much gratitude to my children, Sara, and Eric, along with their spouses, Jennifer, and Mark, for putting up with my barrage of questions to you. Early in the process, you had no idea why I kept asking you what you knew and then reversing your questions and asking you to further explain your answers. I could sense your frustration, but am so grateful you still played along. Over the years you have become more tolerant. Thanks.

I also want to thank my grandchildren for their input into the content. They are getting old enough and astute enough for that input to matter. Also, thank you for indulging me when I pestered you on name choices and cover choices.

I cannot express enough gratitude to a group of people who have been so important in writing this book and previous books. When I have asked them if they would do me a favor, they were gracious while I was talking with them, so I did not hear the comments such as oh no, not again, I am quite sure must have been there. I am so incredibly grateful to you for your quick and informative responses.

Fern Pham is a remarkably busy mother, business lady, and student, who still found the time to give me her timely and valuable insight. Thank you, Fern for giving some of your limited time to me. My sister and brother-in-law have never said no and have been so encouraging. Thank you, Debbie, and Wayne Buck. Thank you, Wayne, for also taking my questions on the phone and not hanging up on me. Cyndi Tingey, what a warrior you have been. Taking the time to print the different chapters so you could respond, was way above and beyond the call. Thank you.

I also want to send out a special thanks to Pastor Greg Young, the host of "Chosen Generation Radio." I have been a guest on his program for several years. Not only did Pastor Greg give me feedback early in the process, but at different times we would have as a basis for our discussion, ideas I was thinking about making a part of the book.

And thank you Andrea Kaye, host of the radio program "The Answer." Thank you for your support and taking the time to meet with me personally. Your feedback and insight were critical. Also, thank you for having me as guest on your program periodically.

TABLE OF CONTENTS

PREFACE

CHAPTERS

1. NATION FOUNDED ON NATURAL RIGHTS

"Among the natural rights of the Colonists are these: First, a right to life; Secondly, to liberty; Thirdly, to property; together with the right to support and defend them in the best manner they can. These are evident branches of, rather than deductions from, the duty of self-preservation, commonly called the first law of nature," is what Samuel Adams wrote in "The Report of the Committee of Correspondence to the Boston Town Meeting" on November 20, 1772.

Committees of Correspondence were intercolonial standing provincial committees. The first of these Committees of Correspondence was formed in November of 1772 in Boston. Committees were not unknown to colonial legislatures in the American colonies, even in he later 1600's. Colonies used these committees to deal with important issues between the individual colony and Britain. Committees were formed in 1764 in Boston to amass opposition to the Currency Act (On September 1, 1764, Parliament passed the Currency Act, effectively assuming control of the colonial currency system. The act prohibited the issue of any new bills and the reissue of existing currency. Parliament favored a "hard currency" system based on the pound sterling, but was not inclined to regulate the colonial bills. Rather, they simply abolished them.) and other reforms imposed on the customs service. In 1765 both Boston and New York City formed committees to oppose the Currency Act. However, unlike the Committees of Correspondence, these early colonial committees were temporary organizations, quickly dissolved after the issue at hand was resolved.

In Boston, on Monday, November 2, 1772, Samuel Adams, Dr. Joseph Warren, James Otis, and other Patriot leaders organized a town meeting at Faneuil Hall in Boston and accumulated enough support to vote in a resolution to create a standing Committee of Correspondence. The purpose of the Boston Committee of Correspondence was to prepare a statement of the rights of the colonists that would be a declaration of the infringement upon the rights of the colonists, and to prepare a letter to be sent to all the towns of Massachusetts and to the world, giving the sense of outrage of the people of Boston.

The United States is an incredibly unique nation. We were the first nation to be founded on the basis of natural rights. Natural rights are rights granted to all people by God. These natural rights cannot be denied or restricted by any government or individual. According to John Locke, Samuel Adams, and Thomas Jefferson, natural rights are defined as life, liberty, and property, or according to Jefferson the pursuit of happiness. Our founders specified many specific liberties in the Bill of Rights when they said congress could not infringe on such liberties as religion, speech, press, assembly, and to petition the government.

The right to life is a gift from God to mankind. An exception we find noted by God, is that when one individual takes the life of another, not in self-defense, then under the law of God and government, the life of the murderer can also be taken. There are few other exceptions. Government therefore would not have the right to establish laws legalizing the destruction of life based on any type of rationalization. Remember, life is not granted by government or man but is an unalienable right that comes from the Creator.

Likewise, liberty is an unalienable right given by the Creator. Government has no right to limit liberty either. But what is liberty?

Merriam-Webster defines liberty as: the quality or state of being free, the power to do as one pleases, freedom from physical restraint, freedom from arbitrary or despotic control, the positive enjoyment of various social, political, or economic rights and privileges, and the power of choice.

Dictionary.com defines liberty as: freedom from arbitrary or despotic government or control, freedom from external or foreign rule; independence, freedom from control, interference, obligation, restriction, hampering conditions, etc.; power or right of doing, thinking, speaking, etc., according to a person's choice, freedom from captivity, confinement, or physical restraint.

According to Collins, liberty is the freedom to live your life in the way that you want, without interference from other people or the authorities.

In all these definitions we have several common threads, but the prevailing thread would be that liberty means to be free from government restraints on how we live our lives and how we think. Government does not control for instance, what vocation we choose, with whom we choose to associate, how we are educated, where we live, how hard we work and how much we are rewarded for that work, to whom we choose to leave our estates, our desires to excel in the arts, athletics or other endeavors, and so many more.

The First Amendment specifically declares that government cannot infringe our liberty of where or when we practice our religion of choice, any form of speech or expression including expression or speech that might be deemed not to be politically correct, our right to report on the activities of the government or what is termed freedom of the press, our right to assemble or with whom we choose to assemble, or our right to petition the government or hold the government responsible. All of these liberties are absolutely essential for a free society. It is these very liberties that an aspiring despot will first try to control.

Our founders, during the Constitutional Convention debated, whether or not the liberties they knew were essential to freedom should be enumerated in the Constitution. They decided against enumerating them because they stated that to enumerate liberties in the document would limit liberty to only those liberties that were enumerated. However, it became necessary to list some of the liberties in order to have the Constitution ratified, and so the first ten amendments, known as the Bill of Rights, were added. So concerned were the founders about having it determined that if a liberty were not listed it would not be a liberty free from government limitations, that James Madison added the catch all Ninth Amendment.

The Ninth Amendment catch all for liberties:

The enumeration in the Constitution, of certain rights, shall not be construed to deny or disparage others retained by the people.

We must always remember that governments only role in natural rights is to protect those rights and not to control or limit those rights. This is the very essence of a free nation. The more government becomes the controller of natural rights, the less freedom the people have and the more tyrannical the government becomes.

The exercise of a liberty by one individual in no way restricts or limits the exercise of that same liberty for another. Because I practice my liberty of free speech, that does not take away from or limit your right of free speech.

My right to a liberty is only restricted when my practice of that liberty in fact infringes on another person's right to that same liberty. An example would be when I use my right to assemble in such a way that by force or other means, I prevent your right to assemble.

The natural right of property, or my right to pursue my happiness, is also a right that comes from the Creator and not from government. This right, as the others, is absolutely critical to an individualist, or a free society. We often times hear the saying that a "person's house is their castle." Property, be it land and buildings, income, rights to copywrites or patents, vehicles, animals, business, or whatever is not the property of government. The assigned role of government is to protect the property of one individual from being taken unlawfully by another. Our Constitution does make one exception, and that is eminent domain or the power of a government to take private property for public use without the owner's consent, provided just compensation is given.

A natural right endowed by the Creator, is not unique to any class, race, sex, or even nationality. All people have these natural rights. Many governments have made the determination, however, that they will not allow natural rights to be exercised, but will instead, through government force, curtail those rights or eliminate them in totality. The United States was the first nation to expressly recognize natural rights, and that they are endowed by the Creator. This recognition, and government performing its proper role of protecting and not controlling these natural rights, is what defines a nation as an individualist nation honoring freedom and liberty, as opposed to a dictatorship that believes it is the right of government to control, curtail, and eliminate these natural rights as it deems.

What is an entitlement?

An entitlement is always based on a government program. There are rules that determine who receives the entitlement. The entitlement or benefit is granted or paid by the government. A necessary criterion of an entitlement is that the government must take from one, generally in the form of taxes, so it can give to another. An entitlement is a form directly or indirectly of sharing wealth, and is associated with collectivism which is an all-encompassing term for Marxism, communism, socialism, progressive, and todays Democrats. The more a nation uses entitlements, the less free are its people and the more tyrannical is the government.

Entitlements are never given without expectations. Entitlements are always given to certain groups or classes of people with the expectation that the recipients of the entitlement will become loyal supporters of those who made the entitlement possible, by voting for that party and or that individual. Those who advocate for the entitlement will justify the entitlement because they will convince the recipient that they deserve the entitlement because they are somehow a victim. Society has somehow brought about their plight and therefore it is society who is responsible for their dilemma or situation and not themselves.

Entitlements always have winners, those who receive what they did not earn, and losers, those who are taxed and accused of being oppressors because they exercised their natural right of aspiring to be and to do the best they could in some chosen endeavor. Entitlements are very often divisive. The group that is penalized so the entitlement can be granted is determined to be the oppressor or the ones who have gained because they somehow purposefully caused the hardship of the receiver. The recipients are told they are victims and their plight in life is not of their own making or choosing, but it is because of some reason such as class, race, or sex.

Entitlements are many times specifically used to cause division. Those who advocate for entitlements, are generally doing so because they desire to bring about a transformation of a society that is an individualist society to a collectivist society for the purpose of controlling all within that society.

In today's America, we are being told that entitlements are rights – health care is a right, education is a right, a house is a right, even televisions and cell phones are rights. Those who claim that entitlements are rights are also the same who would claim that government is the grantor and controller of all rights, be they natural rights or entitlements. The more natural rights are considered to be properly controlled by government, and the more entitlements are accepted as rights with the government having as its proper role to determine who has what, the more collectivist – Marxist, communist, socialist, progressive – that society becomes. This in turn means less freedom the people have and the more dictatorial the government becomes.

Natural rights free the people from the tyranny of government, while entitlements enslave the people to government as government becomes more and more dictatorial, which generally means more and more tyrannical.

2. A REPUBLIC NOT A DEMOCRACY

The story goes that when Benjamin Franklin was asked what our new nation was, he replied, "A Republic, if you can keep it."

The founders did understand the differences between a republic and a democracy, and they purposefully chose a republic.

Alexander Hamilton asserted, "We are now forming a Republican form of government. Real liberty is not found in the extremes of democracy, but in moderate governments. If we incline too much to democracy we shall soon shoot into a monarchy, or some other form of a dictatorship."

A very key point to notice is that a democracy shall soon shoot into a monarchy or some other form of dictatorship. We can safely gather from this, that Hamilton understood that a democracy was as much a form of a dictatorship as is a monarchy. The only difference is the number in the dictator group.

Thomas Jefferson declared: "A democracy is nothing more than mob rule, where fifty-one percent of the people may take away the rights of the other forty-nine."

John Adams, our second president, wrote: "Remember, democracy never lasts long. It soon wastes, exhausts, and murders itself."

James Madison, the father of the Constitution, wrote in Federalist Paper No. 10 that pure democracies, "have ever been spectacles of turbulence and contention; have ever been incompatible with personal security or the rights of property; and have in general been as short in their lives as they have been violent in their deaths."

The Constitution itself, in Article IV, Section 4, declares: "The United States shall guarantee to every State in this Union a Republican Form of Government."

We have been given ample warning that democracies lead to tyranny. Our Founders, in their wisdom, never intended our nation to devolve into a democracy. So, why does this distinction between the forms, "republic" and "democracy" matter? Perhaps because, ignorance of our own history has made it easier for collectivists

(Marxists, communists, socialists, progressives -- all virtually the same) to blur distinctions that have traditionally defined our Republic. When Americans are oblivious of our history and the changes that are slowly being made, they would naturally have little interest in defending the Founders` original intent. The transformation the collectivist seeks, is the "total rejection of the principles and policies on which America was founded, including us being founded as a Republic, by using the word democracy."

Collectivists have effectively begun to convert our republican system that preserves unalienable and individual rights to an increasingly socialist system that replaces the individual`s rights with government distributed entitlements. Sadly, on many counts, collectivists have been successful in this transformation.

A republic is a form of government in which the people are sovereign (ultimate source of power), and give their consent to representatives to make laws. In a republic, the will of the people is filtered through several steps, making it less likely that the majority can endanger the rights of certain individuals or groups. In Federalist #10, Madison explained why a republic, or system of representation, is the form of government best suited to protecting the rights of all. Madison noted that the Constitution's structure and limitations on power created a republic that would "refine and enlarge the public views, by passing them through the medium of a chosen body of citizens, whose wisdom may best discern the true interest of their country, and whose patriotism and love of justice will be least likely to sacrifice it to temporary or partial considerations."

One form of circumventing the specific requirement of republic requiring that laws be made by the representatives of the people, is the call to allow referendums by direct popular vote. This has become common in some states, most notably California. The implementation of direct democracy through Initiative and Referendum not only subverts our system of representative government, but also destroys the checks and balances necessary to preserve our republic.

The fact that such a proposition is not immediately rejected, whether on a statewide basis or on a national basis, is proof that most Americans are misinformed about the nature and character of our system of government. They do not understand the thinking behind the structure of our Constitutional Republic and the protections it provides. This widespread ignorance of our political heritage presents a serious threat to the rights of every American citizen and our future security as a nation of free people.

The Constitution is the centerpiece of American government. Although the framers included democratic elements in our system of government, such as voters directly electing their representatives, our nation is not a democracy. The United States is a Constitutional Republic.

Remember, in a republic, law making powers are not exercised directly by the people but by representatives elected by the people and accountable to them through elections.

Thomas Jefferson affirmed this when he stated, "Modern times...discovered the only device by which rights can be secured, to wit: government by the people, acting not in person but by representatives chosen by themselves."

It is interesting to note that during the Constitutional Convention of 1787, not one voice was raised in support of direct democracy. Indeed, direct democracy was not merely disliked by our Founding Fathers, it was feared as a harbinger of tyranny. They understood that among the fatal flaws of pure democracy is that it provides no checks and balances on the people themselves. Pure democracy has been called tyranny of the majority because it would allow 51% of the people to deprive the other 49% of their rights by a majority vote. Karl Marx referred to this form of government as **"Dictatorship by the Proletariat."**

Again, James Madison told us in Federalist #10, "democracies have ever been spectacles of turbulence and contention; have ever been found incompatible with personal security or the rights of property; and have in general been as short in their lives as they have been violent in their deaths."

The framers designed our system of government so that our God-given rights, those unalienable rights of life, liberty, and property or per the Declaration of Independence, your right to the pursuit of happiness, would be secured and that legislation which affects many would be based on deliberate considerations of the issues by our elected representatives, not on the ever-changing winds of public opinion.

As Alexander Hamilton said, "It had been observed that a pure democracy if it were practicable would be the most perfect government. Experience has proved that no position is more false than this. The ancient democracies in which the people themselves deliberated never possessed one good feature of government. Their very character was tyranny."

If we are to be intellectually honest regarding the efficacy of direct democracy, we must recognize the following:

1. The voting public works full-time to put bread on the table and simply does not have, nor will they make the time to invest in full consideration of issues.

2. Direct democracy can be, and is easily exploited by special interest groups and industries for their own political agenda. It is often easier to manipulate public opinion through the use of mass

media than to go through the time-consuming process of supporting candidates and lobbying them for the legislation they want.

3. In any significant political battle, money is usually the dominant factor. The public is far more influenced by 30 second sound-bite ads or bumper stickers than comprehensive reasoned arguments. This will place an even greater amount of power in the hands of the media, those concerned with distortion, and those with the financial resources to place issues on a ballot and buy advertising time. Let us face it, many of the American people still think Franklin Roosevelt did a "good job" as president, both as a domestic president and a war president. An accurate knowledge of Roosevelt's economic failures and his decisions to accommodate Stalin leads to a different judgement.

4. Minority interests are more likely to come out on the short end of the stick in a direct democracy environment. The fact of the matter is that the majority is often wrong. Our system of government was designed to ensure that the rights of the minority would not be trampled on by the majority.

Decisions made purely on the basis of the "will" of the majority will, at some point strip the minority of their rights.

However, this does not negate the reality that a whole lot of people are rightfully upset by what our elected representatives are doing. The proper solution is not more "democracy." Keep this simple fact in mind; the representatives that you may hold in contempt were themselves elected by popular vote.

This cuts right to the heart of the matter. If you do not like what your representatives are doing once in office, the solution is not to undermine our system of government, but rather to elect better representatives! To really change what is happening in government, better alternatives are needed at the ballot box. People need to change both their vote and where they invest their political support along with informing themselves as to what the issues are and what the people for whom they are voting really believe. We must hold our representatives accountable to us and to their oath of office by requiring adherence to the power limits of the Constitution. The future of our children, grandchildren, and indeed the nation, depends on it.

Our Founders determined that the new nation they had just founded would be a Republic and not a democracy. They were very definite in their choice. Yet, today we have people of all political persuasions referring to our nation as a democracy more than it is referred to as a republic. Our schools indoctrinate our children by telling them we are a democracy and not teaching the differences between democracy and republic. It is especially important that all Americans understand the differences and why our Founders were so definite about the United States being a Republic. Here are some critical differences.

The definition of a democracy is a nation under the rule of the majority. In a democracy, an individual, and any group of individuals composing a minority, have no protection against the power of the majority. In some variations of democracy, people may elect representatives. A republic is similar to a representative democracy, except a republic has a written constitution enumerating basic rights that protect the minority from being completely unrepresented or abused by the majority. I have detailed these protected rights for all, even members of the minority, in "Two Visions of America."

The typical social structure for a democracy is meant to resist segregation by class, politically or economically. Class distinctions can become pronounced, regardless of the economic system; capitalist or socialist. Republics are also meant to resist segregation by class, politically or economically. Class distinctions most often will develop because of the protection of the individual liberty to property, or as stated in the Declaration of Independence, the liberty to pursue happiness.

The economic system of a democracy tends to be a free-market economy, especially in the early days of the democracy. What we learn is that as the people recognize they can vote themselves benefits; many democracies become big welfare states that tend to morph into socialist economies with central planning. Republics are almost always free-market economies or capitalist nations. Typically, the more a republic takes on the characteristics of a democracy, the more it tends to become a welfare state that morphs into a socialist economy with central planning.

Freedom of religion in a democracy is most often protected in the early stages of the democracy. As the majority faction becomes more and more homogeneous in their belief, including Secularism or Atheism, the majority will limit religious freedom for the minority. In a republic, religious freedom is permitted and protected, especially insofar as there is a constitutional prohibition on interfering with freedom of religion for all including a minority.

Free choice most often becomes limited in a democracy. Individuals may make decisions for themselves except insofar as the majority restricts certain choices or all choices that do not conform to the dictates of the majority. In a republic, the individuals may make decisions for themselves, especially insofar as there is a constitutional prohibition on interfering with freedom of choice.

Private property is permitted in a democracy until the majority places limits on property rights on any or all property rights of the minority. In a republic, private property is permitted for all individuals, especially insofar as there is a constitutional prohibition on interfering with property rights.

Discrimination in a democracy is generally not permitted initially. In theory, all citizens have an equal say and so are treated equally. However, over time a democracy becomes a tyranny of the majority over the minority and rights of the minority are eliminated along with a pretense of equality. In a republic, all citizens have an equal say and so are treated equally by the government, especially insofar as there is a constitutional prohibition on government discrimination.

The United States of America is a Democratic Republic. We have a written constitution that is the "Monarch" or the ultimate law of the land. Thus, the United States is governed by rule of law, and not arbitrary law, that is law dependent on the will or wishes of a single person, a small group of people, or the majority of people. In any dispute over the law or the rights of people, the United States Constitution is the final arbiter. That we are a Republic under rule of law is clearly stated in the Constitution where it defines the United States as a Republic, Article 4, Section 4 of the U.S.

Constitution. America's founders were wary of aristocracy and monarchy, where arbitrary law prevails.

In a Republic, an official set of fundamental laws, like the United States Constitution, which includes the Bill of Rights, prohibits the government from limiting or taking away certain "unalienable" rights of the people, even if that government was freely chosen by a majority of the people. In a democracy, the voting majority has limitless power over the minority.

3. TRANSFORMATION

Socialism is just one step in a societal "theory of evolution" submitted by Karl Marx. This theory explains how human society developed over time. In the Communist Manifesto we read, "The history of all hitherto existing society is the history of class struggles. Freeman and slave, patrician and plebian, lord and serf, guild-master and journeyman, in a word, oppressor and oppressed, stood in constant opposition to one another, carried on an uninterrupted, now hidden, now open fight, a fight that each time ended, either in a revolutionary reconstitution of society at large, or in the common ruin of the contending classes."

According to Marx's theory, called "historical materialism," the purpose of socialism is to destroy capitalism, so that society can "progress" to its next evolutionary stage: communism. Karl Marx saw capitalism as a progressive historical stage that would eventually stagnate due to internal contradictions and be followed by socialism. Marxists define capital as "a social, economic relation" between people (rather than between people and things). In this sense they seek to abolish capital. They believe that private ownership of the means of production enriches capitalists (owners of capital) at the expense of workers. In brief, they argue that the owners of the means of production exploit the workforce, or they are the oppressor and the workers are the oppressed.

In Karl Marx's view, the dynamic of capital would eventually impoverish the working class and thereby create the social conditions for a revolution. Private ownership over the means of production and distribution was seen as creating a dependence of non-owning classes on the ruling class, and ultimately as a source of restricting human freedom.

Marxists have offered various related lines of argument, claiming that capitalism is a contradiction-laden system characterized by recurring crises, such as damaging economic depressions that have a tendency towards increasing economic hardships on the workers. They have argued that this tendency of the economic system to unravel, combined with an unjust socialization process that links workers in a worldwide market, create the proper conditions for revolutionary change. Capitalism is seen as just one stage in the evolution of the economic system.

Marx said it would be these conditions that would set the stage for a revolutionary overthrow of capitalism that would lead to socialism, before eventually transforming into communism after class antagonisms and the state cease to exist. In the twentieth, and now the twenty first centuries, we are witnessing social democratic and labor parties, as well as democratic socialists, who seek change through existing democratic channels instead of revolution, and believe that capitalism should be regulated rather than abolished immediately. This is referred to as transformation, a term used by Marx himself when he said that it would be the means by which Great Britain and the United States would move from capitalism to socialism.

Marxist theory states that this period between capitalism and communism, or the period known as socialism, brought about by revolution or through transformation, would be a period where all of society would be under the totalitarian rule of the majority proletariat class known as the "The Dictatorship Of The Proletariat." Communism would follow. Communism is the strictly theoretical system imagined by Karl Marx in which all of society, all of economics, and all politics are combined into one, perfect, classless, automatic, government-less system based on common ownership of all economic means of production, and social sameness. This would be what Marx referred to as a classless society that would be totally conforming and totally equal.

The call for society to be transformed from capitalism to socialism to communism has been heard for quite some time in the United States, and the warnings have been sounded.

In 1956, Mr. Herbert Armstrong wrote about how Russia (the Soviet Union) was waging a new kind of war against America, "a psychological warfare of propaganda, infiltration, subversion, demoralization. It is a warfare that has attacked our minds, our moral and spiritual values, rather than our bodies and our earthly possessions."

Mr. Armstrong explained how this warfare works: "It's a kind of warfare we don't understand or know how to cope with. It uses every diabolical means to weaken us from within, sapping our strength, perverting our morals, sabotaging our educational system, wrecking our social structure, destroying our spiritual and religious life, weakening our industrial and economic power, demoralizing our armed forces, and finally, after such infiltration, overthrowing our government by force and violence!"

More recently we have heard for renewal of these efforts to transform the United State.

"We are going to have to change our conversation; we're going to have to change our traditions, our history; we're going to have to move into a different place as a nation." — Michelle Obama, May 14, 2008

"We are five days away from fundamentally transforming the United States of America." — Barack Obama, October 30, 2008

The change and transformation specifically called for by Michele Obama and Barack Obama is the exact same transformation promised many times by Karl Marx and described by Mr. Armstrong.

"But Communism abolishes all long-standing principles, it abolishes all morality, and it abolishes all religion, instead of constituting them on a new basis." Communist Manifesto, Karl Marx

"Between capitalist and communist society there lies the period of the revolutionary transformation of the one into the other. Corresponding to this is also a political transition period in which the state can be nothing but the revolutionary dictatorship of the proletariat." Critique of the Gotha Program Karl Marx

"The education of all children, from the moment that they can get along without a mother's care, shall be in state institutions." — Karl Marx

"Education is free. Freedom of education shall be enjoyed under the condition fixed by law and under the supreme control of the state" — Das Kapital Karl Marx

The end result of this transformation is to bring about the classless society sought by Marx, a society that would be totally conforming and totally equal. This is to what Michelle Obama is eluding when she says we will have to change our traditions, our history. Marx tells us what traditions we will have to change, and Marx also tells us how we will have to change our history.

Marx said that the family must be abolished. In the Communist Manifesto we read, "Abolition of the family! Even the most radical flare up at this infamous proposal of the Communists. On what foundation is the present family, the bourgeois family, based? On capital, on private gain. In its completely developed form this family exists only among the bourgeois. But, this state of things finds its compliment in the practical absence of the family among the proletarians, and in public prostitution. The bourgeois family will vanish as a matter of course when its complement vanishes, and both will vanish with the vanishing of capital. Do you charge us with wanting to stop the exploitation of children by their parents? To this crime we plead guilty."

To destroy the family was also a major goal of Lenin. Anyone who knows anything about the Bolshevik revolution knows it attacked marriage, family, morality, and especially sexual morality. They knew that if the family could be decimated and sexual morality normalized, it would be much easier for the Bolsheviks to take control.

One of Lenin's first steps to destroy the family was to "liberalize" family relationships that at the same time undermined the influence of the Russian Orthodox Church.

As early as 1917, the new Soviet government passed decrees "On Civil Marriage, Children, and Registries" and "On Dissolution of Marriages." The decree "On Dissolution of Marriages" granted spouses unconditional freedom to a divorce, performed by a local court, at the desire of either one or both parties. "On Civil Marriage" decreed that all except civil marriage (including religious marriage) would cease to be recognized by the state, while at the same time abolishing all distinction between legitimate and illegitimate children.

The 1918 Family Code introduced a whole new morality. In its provisions for divorce, the new legislation granted spouses rights to separate property and thereby abolished shared, family property. Adoption was outlawed, replacing it with a system of state-appointed foster caretakers. The Soviets were also the first government to proclaim complete freedom to abortion.

The Bolsheviks could be called the forerunners of the American Feminist movement. Russian Communists thought the liberation of women required destroying family households. Writing in 1919, Lenin argued that "true liberation of women, true Communism comes about only when and where the masses rise up . . . against . . . small-scale households."

In the 1920 work "The ABC of Communism," Nikolay Bukharin and Yevgeni Preobrazhensky, ideologues of the new order, wrote: "In a bourgeois society, a child is viewed as being exclusively, or at the very least, largely a property of his parents. When parents speak of a child as 'their daughter, their son,' it implies not only their parenthood, but also the right to educate their own children. From a Socialist point of view, this right is entirely and completely unfounded. An individual does not belong to itself, but to society – humankind."

This view is seconded by Lenin, writing in 1920: "We are serious in delivering on our manifesto commitment to transfer the economic and educational functions of the individual household to the society."

The new ideologues explicitly stated the need to destroy the family. A. M. Kollontay, one of the Communist party's most active family policy makers, formulated this need in no uncertain terms as far back as 1918: "The family is doomed. It will be destroyed." N. Bukharin also wrote that "in a Communist society, when private property and oppression of women finally come to an end, so, too, will prostitution and marriage."

As a natural consequence of the new authorities' antifamily policy, a rapid disintegration of the family followed. Freedom of divorce led to serial polygamy, and prostitution masquerading as marriage. In 1920 Petrograd (now St Petersburg), 41% of marriages lasted only three to six months, 22% less than two months, and 11% less than one month. Open prostitution was rampant.

The number of divorces skyrocketed. The state widely advocated freedom of sexual relations. One can say with certainty that the period dealt the natural family a devastating blow, one from which Russian family policy is still recovering.

Marx said all religion, along with morality must be abolished. The Bolsheviks began the process by issuing their first religious policy decrees within months of seizing power, by nationalizing church lands and secularizing the registration of births, deaths, and marriages. In January of 1918 they issued their defining decree, "On the Separation of Church from State and School from Church." Its main effects were to remove the church's status as a legal entity, forbid it from owning property, and to ban formal religious education.

Again, we find Nikolai Bukharin and Yevgeny Preobrazhensky at the forefront as they set out a lasting vision of the Bolshevik's anti-religious mission in their book, The ABC of Communism: "'Religion is the opium of the people,' said Karl Marx. It is the task of the Communist Party to make this comprehensible to the widest possible circles of the laboring masses."

Communists would fight religion on two main fronts: "On the one hand, we have the struggle with the church, as a special organization existing for religious propaganda, materially interested in the maintenance of popular ignorance and religious enslavement. On the other hand, we have the struggle with the widely diffused and deeply ingrained prejudices of the majority of the working population."

Marx also stated that eternal truths, eternal values, and eternal principles must be abolished. Much of this would be accomplished with the abolition of family and religion, but those truths of the natural rights of individuals must also be abolished from society. In April 1917, Lenin restated the old Bolshevik slogan of a "democratic dictatorship of the proletariat and peasantry," to "all power to the soviets" that established the "Dictatorship of the Proletariat."

Dictatorship under the guise of democracy or rule by the majority had been instituted. Censorship along with a one-party press became the norm, and what was considered to be hate speech was outlawed. The government, under the strict control of the Bolshevik party was the final word on all disputes. Those who opposed or objected were violently attacked when they tried to assemble or when they tried to voice any opposition. The natural rights of life, liberty, and property were now under the firm control of the Bolshevik party.

The actions taken by Lenin and the Bolsheviks, documented above, were not unique to the Russian Revolution, but became the road map that other collectivist revolutions followed. When we look at what is happening in the United States today, we see the collectivists within the United States following the same road map.

We have had and continue to have an assault on the family. The collectivists state that you must support murder of an unborn child, and yes even of a newly born child, if you wish to be a part of them. Divorce is made easier and easier and has become widely accepted. Pornography is now considered to be protected speech. Promiscuity is not frowned upon but instead is being glorified in many sectors of our society. We are telling our children that which is prohibited by Biblical teaching, is normal and even desired.

Morality and religious beliefs that stress right and wrong, and good and bad, are considered to be "old school" and are considered by many to be racist, sexist, homophobic, and narrow minded. We are now being bombarded in every aspect of entertainment and communication that all is good so long as "nobody gets hurt." The hurt part is often sacrificed for the sake of "being open minded." The long-standing axiom of the collectivist, "The ends always justify the means" has now been extended to all aspects of society and not just applied to the political element.

Our nations long standing principles of eternal truths and values that are outlined in our founding documents, The Declaration of Independence, The United States Constitution, and the Bill of Rights, are being ridiculed, demonized, and minimized. We are being told by the collectivists that these principles are outdated and no longer apply. Some collectivists are now putting forth the idea that these principles were never applicable as sound principles, truths, and values, because our founders were racist and sexist.

The basic principles declared in these documents that we were told were critical to freedom and liberty, are being totally reversed if they have not already been. We were told that "rule of law," where all were treated equally under the law regardless of economic, social, or political, position, must always reign supreme. More and more we are seeing the law being applied differently to different people especially because of political position or political beliefs.

The principle that we must have a limited government, even to the point that the powers of the federal government were enumerated in the United States Constitution and then reinforced in the Tenth Amendment within the Bill of Rights, was critical if we were to not again come under the tyranny of government. Today we cannot find one facet of our lives that does not have some form of government control, and we are told that even more government control is necessary.

The principle of divided government was critical to protect us from one branch of government assuming all the power, and thus acting as a tyrant as it assumes the roles of the other branches.

The Judicial Branch today rules on the law, makes the law, and tells the executive how they must execute the law. The Judicial Branch, which was not to be a political branch, that is why judges were to be appointed for life, gives more and more rulings based on political beliefs and not on the words in the United States Constitution or the law.

We were a unique country in so many ways, but probably none more unique than the principle of "sovereignty of the people." As Benjamin Franklin stated, this meant that the people would be the superior and the government would be the servant. Every time a law is passed, or a regulation becomes affective, the government has gained more power and the people have surrendered more sovereignty and freedom.

Remember, we were told that we were being transformed. Yes, we were told we would be transformed from a nation under rule of law, limited government, divided government, where the people are the sovereign, and where our natural rights are endowed to us by our Creator and not man nor government, to a nation under arbitrary law as determined by a sovereign government, where government is all controlling of our lives and our thoughts, where all power is in the Judicial Branch of government, where the government is sovereign and we are servants to that government, and where government becomes the controller of our life, liberty, and property.

Marx said the United States would not have a revolution but would go through a transformation as it moved from a capitalist society, to a socialist society, and ultimately to a communist society.

4. MANIFESTO TRANSFORMATION

From the Communist Manifesto:

"The Communist revolution is the most radical rupture with traditional property relations: no wonder that its development involves the most radical rupture with traditional ideas.

But let us have done with the bourgeoise objections to Communism.

We have seen above that the first step in the revolution by the working class is to raise the proletariat to the position of the ruling class, to win the battle of democracy.

The proletariat will use its political supremacy to wrest, by degrees, all capital from the bourgeoisie, to centralize all instruments of production in the hands of the State, that is of the proletariat organized as the ruling class; and to increase the total of productive forces as rapidly as possible.

Of course, in the beginning, this cannot be effected except by means of despotic inroads on the rights of property, and on the conditions of bourgeois production: by means of measures, therefore, which appear economically insufficient and untenable, but which, in the course of the movement outstrip themselves, necessitate further inroads upon the old social order, and are unavoidable as a means of entirely revolutionizing the mode of production.

These measures will of course be different in different countries.

Nevertheless, in the most advanced countries, the following will be pretty generally applicable:

1. Abolition of property in land and application of all rents of land to public purposes.
2. A heavy progressive or graduated income tax.
3. Abolition of all right of inheritance.
4. Confiscation of the property of all emigrants and rebels.
5. Centralization of credit in the hands of the State, by means of a national bank with State capital and an exclusive monopoly.

6. Centralization of the means of communication and transport in the hands of the State.
7. Extension of factories and instruments of production owned by the State; the bringing into cultivation of wastelands, and the improvement of the soil generally in accordance with a common plan.
8. Equal liability of all to labor. Establishment of industrial armies, especially for agriculture.
9. Combination of agriculture with manufacturing industries: gradual abolition of the distinction between town and country, by a more equable distribution of the population over the country.
10. Free education for all children in public schools. Abolition of children's factory labor in its present form. Combination of education with industrial production."

The Communist Manifesto is about defining how relationships between people have been transformed over the years. Marx and Engels stated the next and final transformation would be the inevitable transformation from capitalism to socialism with the ultimate end being the harmonious, classless, conforming, and equal state of communism. How have the collectivists been able to implement these ten measures to bring about the transformation from capitalism to socialism?

Abolition of property in land and application of all rents of land to public purposes. After the transformation, land would no longer be owned by individual people but would be considered common property or owned by the government. People who made income by renting the land they owned to others, would no longer exist. The government might still charge rent for the use of land, but that rent would be another source of income for the government to be redistributed as they thought would be best.

This is where eminent domain comes into the picture, and even property taxes. Once you own your property outright by paying off your mortgage, you still do not technically own it because the government could raise property taxes so high that it makes it unaffordable to retain.

Eminent domain has always been reserved for the government to take private property because it was considered necessary for public use, such as a freeway. The right of eminent domain has been expanded however, when a 2005 Supreme Court decision opened up a more complex legal area: the government's ability to take private land and give it to another private entity, such as a corporation.

A heavy progressive or graduated income tax. When Marx and Engels wrote the Communist Manifesto in 1848, the United States of America had never had an income tax. In order to help pay for its war effort in the American Civil War, Congress imposed its first personal income tax in 1861. It was part of the Revenue Act of 1861 (3% of all incomes over US$800; rescinded in 1872). In 1894 Congress passed the Wilson-Gorman tariff which was an income tax at the rate of 2% for income over $4,000. It was overturned by the Supreme Court in 1895 when they determined the income tax law violated the United States Constitution.

in 1913 the Sixteenth Amendment was ratified and became a part of the Constitution, thus granting Congress the power to collect taxes on personal income. The top tax rate was 7%. By 1916 the top rate had been increased to 67% and was 77% in 1918. In 1944, the top rate peaked at 94%.

The American people are constantly told that the rates must be fair and just. Yet, when the question of what is fair and just is asked, the answer is, "we are not quite sure, but we know it must be higher."

In April of 1942 we learned what is thought to be fair and just. Franklin Roosevelt proposed a 100% top tax rate on all taxable income over $25,000 (1942 dollars). Roosevelt told Congress, "no American citizen ought to have a net income, after he has paid his taxes, of more than $25,000 a year, the 100% rate is fair and just."

Abolition of all rights of inheritance. The Revenue Act of 1916 contained an estate tax with many features of today's system. From 1932 until 2002, the top rate exceeded 50% of the estate. It was 70% or higher from 1935 to 1981, reaching its highest level of 77% 1941 to 1976.

When Jenny Marx (Jenny was the wife of Karl Marx) mother died, she received a meaningful inheritance. Nothing was given to anybody else, but the funds were used so Karl and Jenny Marx could live for a while, more like the upper class they knew as children. When Karl Marx mother died, he received an even larger inheritance than did his wife. Again, nothing was given to anybody else. The funds were used so Karl and Jenny Marx could live more like the upper class they knew as children.

Confiscation of the property of all emigrants and rebels. Today we euphemistically refer to this measure of the Communist Manifesto as government seizures, tax liens, or "forfeiture." Public "law" 99-570 (1986) also referred to as "Antidrug Abuse Act of 1986"; Executive order 11490, sections 1205, 2002 which gives private land to the Department of Urban Development; or the IRS confiscation of property without due process. The civil asset forfeiture law allows government agencies like the IRS or the Department of Justice to confiscate anyone's property without obtaining criminal charges against them.

The Marx intent of this was more as a practical step intended not so much to aid the state in its drive toward public ownership, but to serve as a warning to the bourgeoisie not to engage in counter-revolutionary activity.

Centralization of credit in the hands of the State, by means of a national bank with State capital and an exclusive monopoly. We call it the Federal Reserve which is a credit/debit system nationally organized by the Federal Reserve act of 1913. All local banks are members of the Fed system, and are regulated by the Federal Deposit Insurance Corporation (FDIC). The Federal Reserve Act of 1913 created our central banking system (the Federal Reserve). Enacted by Woodrow Wilson, the idea was to reform the banking and the currency system. The objectives included prevention of financial panics with the ready availability of cash from a money reserve, an expanding-contracting money supply to match the state of the economy, and a new currency - the federal reserve note. It failed miserably to prevent financial panics in 1929 and again in 2008. Many banks failed in the years following 1929. In 2008 the federal government directly rescued many banks because of the banks being forced to make bad real estate loans by federal regulations and by greatly relaxing any semblance to sound underwriting practices.

In an article in Forbes on July 14, 2015 by Michael Collins, we read, "Most people think that the big bank bailout was the $700 billion that the treasury department used to save the banks during the financial crash in September of 2008. But this is a long way from the truth because the bailout is still ongoing. The Special Inspector General for TARP summary of the bailout says that the total commitment of government is $16.8 trillion dollars with the $4.6 trillion already paid out. Yes, it was trillions not billions and the banks are now larger and still too big to fail. The operating principles of the big banks is a cesspool of greed, ethics and criminal intent and they give a bad name to free market capitalism. During the housing bubble, Wall Street was considered the heart and soul of free market capitalism, but when the banks were in danger of total collapse they fell on their knees as socialists, begging the government and taxpayers to bail them out."

The federal government today has a monopoly on the student loan sector. This control has led to a student debt crisis. The government now controls 80% of the market, and private banking institutions cannot compete with federal student loans. As it stands now, the government has seemingly endless capital to loan, boasts lower interest rates than private institutions, gives deferments and forbearances on loans, and even offers partial loan forgiveness. The government has become too willing to hand out crippling loans that saddle young Americans in debt. The federal government has abandoned any use of underwriting criteria and the student loan program has become what Marx and Engels had in mind: that is that the bank would freely grant credit and then have the control to determine if repayment would or would not be required. The student loan program has become a prime example of how centralized credit was intended to work and does work; anybody can get a loan and anybody or all can have that loan forgiven.

From the viewpoint of Marx, this measure would deprive financiers of both their wealth and their power to direct the economy. With exclusive control of credit facilities, the state would decide what parts of the economy should be expanded and by how much. It will also enable the state to finance the "national workshops" that Marx envisioned.

Centralization of the means of communication and transport in the hands of the State. In our capitalist nation, communication and transportation are controlled and regulated by the Federal Communications Commission (FCC) established by the Communications Act of 1934 and the Department of Transportation and the Interstate Commerce Commission (established by Congress in 1887), and the Federal Aviation Administration as well as Executive orders 11490, 10999 -- not to mention various state bureaucracies and regulations. There is also the federal postal monopoly, AMTRAK, and CONRAIL -- outright socialist (government-owned) enterprises. Instead of free-market private enterprise in these important industries, these fields in America are semi-cartelized through the government's regulatory-industrial complex.

Fairness doctrine was a United States communications policy (1949–87) that was formulated by the Federal Communications Commission (FCC). It required licensed radio and television broadcasters to present what the FCC considered fair and balanced coverage of controversial issues (per the definition of the FCC) of interest to their communities, including by devoting equal airtime to opposing points of view.

After 1987, primarily radio, became driven by advertising dollars, as you would expect in a capitalist system, and conservative radio programs began to dominate. Senator Feinstein believed that talk radio had become one-sided and "explosive." She said it "pushes people, I think, to extreme views without a lot of information."

When Feinstein was asked if she supported a return of the Fairness Doctrine, she said "I am looking at it, as a matter of fact. I do believe in fairness. I remember when there was a fairness doctrine, and I think there was much more serious correct reporting to people."

Marx saw this measure as a means of depriving a few capitalists of their power to control a nation's economy, and it would allow the state to develop its internal communication system on the basis of social need, as did Feinstein with the Fairness Doctrine. Regarding transportation, Marx saw another immediate result would be that all transportation would be made free to the poor.

Extension of factories and instruments of production owned by the State; the bringing into cultivation of wastelands, and the improvement of the soil generally in accordance with a common plan. The United States has a significant degree of government involvement in agriculture in the form of price support subsidies and acreage allotments and land-use controls. The Desert Entry Act and The Department of Agriculture, the Department of Commerce and Labor, Department of Interior, the Environmental Protection Agency, Bureau of Land Management, Bureau of Reclamation, Bureau of Mines, National Park Service, and the IRS control business through corporate regulations.

Today the Bureau of Land Management (BLM) manages approximately 245 million acres. Laws and regulations of the federal government govern livestock and poultry, crop production, drinking water, farm facilities fuel and equipment, buildings/construction/renovation, wastes, air emissions, and chemical handling to name a few.

We know of the EPA for instance suing a farmer because the farmer dug a pond on his land to water his cattle while another farmer was sued for, and then stopped from plowing their land.

It is estimated that federal rules and regulations cost American businesses $1.75T per year, and we have calls for even more laws, regulations, and rules on our businesses.

In a 2015 Senate Judiciary Committee hearing, one senator noted that "The Federal Register indicates there are over 430 departments, agencies, and sub-agencies in the federal government." In searching for a definitive answer to know how many departments, agencies, and sub agencies there are, the most consistent answer was that nobody knows for sure.

Equal liability of all to labor. Establishment of industrial armies, especially for agriculture. Americans call it Minimum Wage that is thought to bring equality to labor. Executive Order 11000 allows the government to mobilize civilians into work brigades under government supervision.

Under communism, the privilege of choosing not to work is abolished. With everyone working, "productive labor ceases to be a class attribute," allowing Marx to claim that communism "recognizes no class differences because everyone is a worker like everyone else."

In calling for the establishment of industrial armies, especially for agriculture, Marx is as concerned with changing the personalities of the people involved as he is with promoting greater economic efficiency.

Combination of agriculture with manufacturing industries: gradual abolition of the distinction between town and country, by a more equable distribution of the population over the country. Executive Order No. 11647 divided the United States into 10 Federal Regional Councils, each controlled by an appointed bureaucrat for the stated purpose of improving coordination of the activities of all levels of government. The 10 federal regions were to be empowered to control all forms of regionalism within the United States. Regional divisions supplementing the 10 federal regions include state subregions, Federal Reserve regions, population regions, and regions to control the land, water, and natural resources of America.

One of the least recognized of the harmful divisions Marx sees in the human species is between man the "restricted town animal" and man the "restricted country animal". We must remember that, for Marx, peasants are a "class of barbarians", whose way of existence he labels the "idiocy of rural life". People in the country, therefore, need the city and all that it represents in the way of advanced technology, culture, and education, just as people living in the city need the country, its fresh air, inspiring scenery, close contact with animals, and toil on the land itself in order to achieve their full stature as human beings.

Free education for all children in public schools. Abolition of children's factory labor in its present form. Combination of education with industrial production. The public-school system has been transformed from a system of education to an indoctrination system under the control of the Federal Government. The United States Constitution never gave the power of education to the Federal Government.

"I believe that education is the civil rights issue of our generation. And if you care about promoting opportunity and reducing inequality, the classroom is the place to start. Great teaching is about so much more than education; it is a daily fight for social justice." Arne Duncan, former Secretary of Education under Barack Obama

"Give me four years to teach the children and the seed I have sown will never be uprooted." Vladimir Lenin

The Marxist belief is that the child does not belong to the parent but is the asset of the state. The parent is not to have any influence over the values of the child. The state will be totally responsible for teaching the child in all aspects, including values and morals. This influence is to begin as early as possible, when the child can be free from the mother. That would be nursery school, and in some instances, earlier.

The Communist Manifesto, written by Karl Marx and Friedrich Engels, remains an essential guidebook for any socialist serious about overthrowing capitalism. The measures discussed in this chapter, are still critical means in this overthrow or transformation. Although some of the societal conditions, such as the disparity between city and rural population, have changed, the basics are still very much the same. The transformation has been implemented in many of the ten, and continues in all. It is critical that those who would not support the overthrow of capitalism understand these measures and their significance, and how so many of the measures Marx said were necessary to bring about the transformation are, or have been partially or totally implemented.

5. LENIN'S DECALOGUE

The study of how Lenin consolidated power is a long and complicated story. Vladimir Ilyich Ulyanov, the person who became known as Lenin to the world, was born to parents who worked in the Tsar's school system. Despite being a part of the Romanov bureaucracy, they raised their children to become rebels. Their oldest son was arrested in a plot to kill Alexander III, and was hung in public with 4 other rebels. Many of us believe this was a driving force that led young Vladimir to not only become a rebel, but also accounts for his hatred of Nicholas II and his family. It also could be the reason that Nicholas and his family were brutally murdered by the Lenin government and not allowed to go to England. Alexandria was known to be a favorite of her grandmother, Queen Victoria.

While looking at the background information on the Russian revolution and the change to a Communist state in Russia, we learn that many of the actions and reforms of the Bolshevik party, or Lenin, closely resemble the very things Karl Marx said were necessary to bring about Marx's classless communist society.

Lenin also closely did what he said was necessary in his Decalogue "Manual to Seize Control of a Society". In 1913, Lenin wrote the "Decalogue" which featured tactical actions to seize power. He used these actions in the 1917 Russian Re-Revolution (The October Surprise), usurping control from the Provincial Government, who were in control after the original Russian Revolution which occurred earlier in the spring of 1917.

1. Corrupt the youth and give them absolute sexual freedom.

2. Infiltrate and take control of the mass communication media.

3. Divide the population into antagonist groups; encourage arguments between them over social issues.

4. Destroy the people's confidence in their leaders.

5. Talk all the time about democracy and republic, but when the opportunity arises, seize power as a dictator.

6. Cooperate with the drainage of public funds; discrediting the image of the country, especially overseas, and create panics within the population through the launching of an inflationary process.

7. Encourage strikes, even if they are illegal, in the country's key industries.

8. Promote riots while conspiring to prevent intervention by law enforcement.

9. Cooperate actively in destroying the moral foundations of society and honesty and trust in the government's promises. Infiltrate other parties with your own people, forcing them to vote for what is useful to your own party's interest.

10. Register everyone who has firearms, in order to confiscate them when the time comes, preventing them from opposing your revolution.

Following the Bolshevik Revolution, Lenin and his new communist government initiated many reforms. They took land from the Tsar, the church, nobles, and other landlords, and redistributed it among the peasants in order to reform the agricultural sector and reward the peasants for their loyalty during the Revolution.

An especially important element of any Marxist society is free education as called for by Marx in the "Communist Manifesto" and discussed in the previous chapter. Lenin began this free education program, not just for children, but also for adults. He realized that adults had been denied education to learn to read and write, so Lenin introduced evening classes for workers. This education included a strong component on communism or a strong indoctrination element. Lenin also knew that with the proper indoctrination he could, "take any individual for four years and have that individual for a lifetime."

A Women's Rights Department, headed by Alexandra Kollontai, a former exile member of the Bolshevik Central committee, was also launched. This department addressed issues like the employment and education of women. A very liberal abortion policy was also instituted as was promiscuity promoted. Husbands and wives were specifically separated, because of work assignments, for long periods of time. Divorce was simplified along with or because of promiscuity being promoted.

During this reform period, the Bolshevik Party changed its name to the Communist Party, and established measures to restrict political opposition. All newspapers that were not state controlled were banned or forced to at least minimize criticism of government policies, but the goal was total elimination of any criticism.

The main opposition Liberal Party, a party that had launched most of the communist leaders, was banned. Lenin had also started his political career in the Liberal Party before his resignation as a result of the teachings of Karl Marx. The Constitutional Democrats were also banned, and its leadership arrested.

A commission to fight counter-revolution and espionage, called Cheka, was established. Cheka was a secret police force that reported directly to Lenin on all illegal or opposition activities against communism. Cheka ensured that people who did not support communism were recommended for expulsion from Russia or imprisoned for life. Cheka's workforce grew to 30, 000 members in a bid to crush all opposition. Moscow became the new capital city in a move based on the belief that it was more central than Petrograd. The Communist Party adopted the same calendar that was followed by Western European countries.

After Lenin had gained control of the Russian government, it was his stated goal as a Bolshevik to extend the revolution throughout the world. His first attempt at this endeavor was to invade Poland, but it failed. He then established the Communist International or Cominterm. He had such success in Russia with his efforts to infiltrate the education system, the media, and the entertainment industry, he determined this would be his goal to gain control of the United States. His success of doing this is discussed in my book "The Road to Tyranny."

Lenin also understood that to be successful with a communist takeover in any society, it was mandatory to destroy the family as a strong unit. (the destruction of the family is a necessary characteristic of the transformation and will be mentioned many times). It was also mandatory to have the state become god to the people.

Never forget that Karl Marx specifically mandated the breakdown of the core family unit, free education so an indoctrination system could be ensured, with the destruction of all long-standing principles, morality, and religion. Lenin, along with Trotsky, was a dedicated student of Marx. How did Lenin bring about these Marxian ideas and how important to these Marxist goals were the ten elements of Lenin's Decalogue? As you go through these items, be sure you remember that Marxists have used the same tactics in all takeovers. Test them against current happenings in the United States.

Corrupt the youth and give them absolute sexual freedom. In the Soviet Union, women's rights became much more sweeping. In addition to universal suffrage, women gained access to higher education, and the right to equal pay. Abortion was legalized, a world-first, and freely available to factory workers. Children, whether born in or out of wedlock, were granted equal status in law. Marriage became secular, divorce was simplified and streamlined, sex outside wedlock was destigmatized, and male homosexuality decriminalized.

Mentioned earlier, Alexandra Kollontai, the first Commissar of Social Welfare and the most prominent woman in the Kremlin government, was the key ideologist of sexual freedom. For Kollontai, the sexual revolution was mainly about mentally liberating women from the expectations of monogamy and servitude to the family. Being able to decide when to have children, she argued, and secure in the knowledge that the state would provide for them, would allow women to study, work, and involve themselves in public affairs.

Kollontai emphasized how the social dominance of love simply reinforced power imbalances between the sexes. "All modern education of a woman is aimed at closing her life in love emotions," she wrote in a 1911 article. "It is time to teach the woman to take love not as the basis of life, but only as a step, as a way to reveal her true self. The new women types," Kollontai wrote, "would know that the treasures of life are not exhausted by love."

Lenin shared Kollontai's condemnation of "bourgeois' conceptions of love." He thought that forsaking all-consuming ideas about marriage would strengthen class solidarity and push workers to commit to implementing a socialist society. In January 1915, Lenin wrote a letter to the revolutionary leader, Inessa Armand, in which he said that love should be free from material and financial worries and calculations — but that unbinding love from raising children, and tacitly encouraging adultery, was 'a bourgeois, not a proletarian demand'. As it happened, Armand was also Lenin's lover.

Lenin understood and stated this, "Destroy the family, you destroy the country."

Infiltrate and take control of the mass communication media. A free and independent press does not have much history in Russia. Control of the media by the government, or communist party, dates back to the very beginning of Lenin's control. The Bolsheviks curtailed freedom of speech and press in Russia from the very beginning. One of the most important initial decrees passed by the Soviet of People's Commissars and signed by

Vladimir Lenin October 27, 1917, was the "Decree on the Press." This Decree essentially outlawed newspapers that published views opposed to the October Revolution. Claiming such papers to be tsarist reactionaries, the Communists closed 319 newspapers from 1917-1918. Additional measures soon followed. A tribunal was established in 1917 to investigate and suppress bourgeois newspapers. Later in 1917, a state monopoly on advertising was instituted, depriving most papers of revenue.

The government (and therefore the party) controlled rights to licensing and financing papers. Appointment to high-level media jobs, such as editors, was controlled by the Communist Party and based on purely political and ideological considerations. According to one study, few Soviet media officials had significant experience working in the individual media they came to control. Training for journalists was completely controlled by governmental institutions and finally, if all else failed, governmental censorship was utilized. Contrary to a common belief that the Soviet Union widely practiced censorship, after an initial period of censorship and repression under Lenin and Stalin, the true controls over a free press were embodied in the close relationship between party officials and the media. Editors willingly made for compliant news outlets that followed the party line.

Divide the population into antagonist groups; encourage arguments between them over social issues. The Tsar had been overthrown. The Provisional Government was in power. Lenin had been in exile. Lenin was granted a special favor to travel through Germany by the German government, so he could return to Russia. World War I was still raging, and Germany was fighting Russia. Lenin returned to Russia on April 3,1917, and announced what became known as the April Theses. As he left the railway station, Lenin was lifted on to one of the armored cars specially provided for such occasions. The atmosphere was electric and enthusiastic.

In his speech, Lenin attacked Bolsheviks for supporting the Provisional Government. Instead, he argued, revolutionaries should be telling the people of Russia that they should take over the control of the country. In his speech, Lenin urged the peasants to take the land from the rich landlords and the industrial workers to seize the factories. Lenin accused those Bolsheviks who were still supporting the government of Prince Georgi Lvov of betraying socialism and suggested that they should leave the party. Lenin ended his speech by telling the assembled crowd that they must "fight for the social revolution, fight to the end, till the complete victory of the proletariat".

Lenin continued to promote class antagonisms between the rich and the poor, the bourgeoisie and proletariat, and of course during the civil war that took place in Russia after the Bolsheviks gained power in October of 1917, between the Whites and the Reds.

"We fully regard civil wars, i.e., wars waged by the oppressed class against the oppressing class, slaves against slave-owners, serfs against landowners, and wageworkers against the bourgeoisie, as legitimate, progressive and necessary." Lenin, Socialism and War

Destroy the people's confidence in their leaders. Lenin wrote, "On the National Pride of the Great Russians," in which he said, "We are full of a sense of national pride, and for that very reason we *particularly* hate *our* slavish past (when the landed nobility led the peasants into war to stifle the freedom of Hungary, Poland, Persia and China), and our slavish present, when these selfsame landed proprietors, aided by the capitalists, are loading us into a war in order to throttle Poland and the Ukraine, crush the democratic movement in Persia and China, and strengthen the gang of Romanovs, Bobrinskys, and Purishkeviches, who are a disgrace to our Great-Russian national dignity. Nobody is to be blamed for being born a slave; but a slave who not only eschews a striving for freedom but justifies and eulogizes his slavery (e.g., calls the throttling of Poland and the Ukraine, etc., a "defense of the fatherland" of the Great Russians)—such a slave is a lickspittle and a boor, who arouses a legitimate feeling of indignation, contempt, and loathing."

This would be paramount to calling the founding fathers a disgrace to our Great-American national dignity. Of course, that is being taught in many American schools today; that is that the founding fathers were horrible slave owners.

Talk all the time about democracy and republic, but when the opportunity arises, seize power as a dictator. Lenin wrote again in, "On the National Pride of the Great Russians," ""No nation can be free if it oppresses other nations, said Marx and Engels, the greatest representatives of consistent nineteenth century democracy, who became the teachers of the revolutionary proletariat. And, full of a sense of national pride, we Great-Russian workers want, come what may, a free and independent, a democratic, republican and proud Great Russia, one that will base its relations with its neighbors on the human principle of equality, and not on the feudalist principle of privilege, which is so degrading to a great nation. Just because we want that, we say: it is impossible, in the twentieth century and in Europe (even in the far east of Europe), to "defend the fatherland" otherwise than by using every revolutionary means to combat the monarchy, the landowners and the capitalists of one's own fatherland, i.e., the worst enemies of our country. We say that the Great Russians cannot "defend the fatherland" otherwise than by desiring the defeat of tsarism in any war, this as the lesser evil to nine-tenths of the inhabitants of Great

Russia. For tsarism not only oppresses those nine-tenths economically and politically, but also demoralizes, degrades, dishonors and prostitutes them by teaching them to oppress other nations and to cover up this shame with hypocritical and quasi-patriotic phrases."

This is paramount to people declaring that the American Republic must be protected at all costs, while at the same time those proclaiming the greatness of the Republic, negate the liberties of the minority and impose more and more government control through laws and regulations.

Cooperate with the drainage of public funds; discrediting the image of the country, especially overseas, and create panics within the population through the launching of an inflationary process. "The best way to destroy the capitalist system is to debauch the currency," Lenin. In other words, incompetent central bankers are a communist's best friend. The idea is hyperinflation breaks down markets and breaks down classes. Business cannot plan beyond today if they do not know what money will be worth tomorrow. And a collapsing currency turns the bourgeoisie into the proletariat overnight. That sound you hear is the revolution coming.

In Lenin's own words, the bourgeois state does not wither away, but is abolished by the proletariat in the course of the revolution. We see the same axiom, "the ends justify the means" or whatever it takes.

Encourage strikes, even if they are illegal, in the country's key industries. Lenin wrote in his article "On Strikes" his theory on the necessity of strikes. "In the first place we must seek an explanation for the outbreak and spread of strikes. Everyone who calls to mind strikes from personal experience, from reports of others, or from the newspapers, will see immediately that strikes break out and spread wherever big factories arise and grow in number. It would scarcely be possible to find a single one among the bigger factories employing hundreds (at times even thousands) of workers in which strikes have not occurred. When there were only a few big factories in Russia there were few strikes; but ever since big factories have been, multiplying rapidly in both the old industrial districts and in new towns and villages, strikes have become more frequent.

Why is it that large-scale factory production always leads to strikes? It is because capitalism must necessarily lead to a struggle of the workers against the employers, and when production is on a large scale the struggle of necessity takes on the form of strikes."

Let us explain this as a Marxist would.

Capitalism is the name given to that social system under which the land, factories, implements, etc., belong to a small number of landed proprietors and capitalists, while the mass of the people possesses no property, or very little property, and is compelled to hire itself out as workers. The landowners and factory owners hire workers and make them produce wares of this or that kind which they sell on the market. The factory owners, furthermore, pay the workers only such a wage as provides a bare subsistence for them and their families, while everything the worker produces over and above this amount goes into the factory owner's pocket, as his profit. Under capitalist economy, therefore, the people in their mass are the hired workers of others, they do not work for themselves but work for employers for wages. It is understandable that the employers always try to reduce wages; the less they give the workers, the greater their profit. The workers try to get the highest possible wage in order to provide their families with sufficient and wholesome food, to live in good homes, and to dress as other people do and not like beggars. A constant struggle is, therefore, going on between employers and workers over wages; the employer is free to hire whatever worker he thinks fit and, therefore, seeks the cheapest. The worker is free to hire himself out to an employer of his choice, so that he seeks the dearest, the one that will pay him the most. Whether the worker works in the country or in town, whether he hires himself out to a landlord, a rich peasant, a contractor, or a factory owner, he always bargains with the employer, fights with him over the wages.

But is it possible for a single worker to wage a struggle by himself? The number of working people is increasing, peasants are being ruined and flee from the countryside to the town or the factory. The landlords and factory owners are introducing machines that rob the workers of their jobs. In the cities there are increasing numbers of unemployed and in the villages, there are more and more beggars; those who are hungry drive wages down lower and lower. It becomes impossible for the worker to fight against the employer by himself. If the worker demands good wages or tries not to consent to a wage cut, the employer tells him to get out, that there are plenty of hungry people at the gates who would be glad to work for low wages.

Strikes, therefore, teach the workers to unite; they show them that they can struggle against the capitalists only when they are united; strikes teach the workers to think of the struggle of the whole working class against the whole class of factory owners and against the arbitrary, police government. This is the reason that socialists call strikes "a school of war," a school in which the workers learn to make war on their enemies for the liberation of the whole people, of all who labor, from the yoke of government officials and from the yoke of capital."

Promote riots while conspire to prevent intervention by law enforcement. The time in Russia from the 1905 Revolution to the takeover by the Bolsheviks in October of 1917, proved to be a time or riots. The time after the Reds (Bolsheviks) gained power proved to be even more bloody as the civil war between the Reds and the Whites occurred.

Mike Carey, in his article "Violence and Terror in the Russian Revolution" gives us an idea of how riotous the times were with each side acting as the law enforcers.

"The February Revolution which deposed the Tsar is often depicted as relatively bloodless, but in fact its casualties were far greater than those of the more famous October Revolution which brought the Bolsheviks to power. On the first days of the revolution in Petrograd, hundreds of marchers were shot by troops defending the old order, and in the chaos, around 1,400 people are thought to have been killed.

Among the high ideals of the Revolution, however, was the creation of a more humane society. The Provisional Government (the government that took power upon the abdication of Nicholas II) quickly abolished the death penalty and granted Russian citizens important new civil rights. Even so, its fortunes would largely be defined by their continued commitment to fighting the war to the finish.

The Provisional Government struggled to deal with the violent forces unleashed by the fall of the autocracy, including factory occupations, mutinies among the armed forces, and violence perpetrated as peasants seized land for themselves away from the landlords.

On top of all this, Russia's position in the World War I was deteriorating. After the disastrous June Offensive – where the then-Minister of War, Alexander Kerensky unsuccessfully tried to restore the Russian army's will to fight – mutinies and desertions from the army grew. Many peasant-soldiers preferred to return to their home villages and take part in the expropriations of land rather than continue to fight in the war, fearing that they would lose out if they stayed on the front lines while land was being redistributed back home.

As the Provisional Government lost its grip on the country, it found itself forced to revive the old violent methods of keeping order, including the reinstatement of the death penalty; in July 1917, it violently repressed a large demonstration of soldiers, sailors and workers. It was in the context of disintegrating state power, various forms of unrest across the country and rising dissatisfaction with the continuing slaughter in the war that the far-left Bolshevik Party gained influence.

So, when the Bolsheviks organized their Red Guards to storm the Winter Palace on October 25th, 1917, there were very few willing to defend it.

Lenin, the leader of the Bolsheviks, wanted to end the war, but not for reasons of pacifism. He believed that violence would continue as long as society was divided into fundamentally opposed social classes, inevitably leading to social conflict, and as long as capitalist governments required imperialism to maintain themselves, inevitably provoking wars between nations.

Class war, Lenin argued, was of all the wars known in history... the only lawful, rightful, just and genuinely great war. He hoped to transform the

First World War from a conflict between nations into a European-wide civil war between classes – between, in his view, the working-class and those who exploited them. The struggle against counter-revolutionary forces was depicted in the terms of a 'just war'.

To win this class war, the Bolsheviks thought it would be necessary to replace the various capitalist states with a working-class dictatorship able to suppress by force any attempts at counter-revolution. More cynical minds suggest that the Bolsheviks were merely aspiring for a dictatorship of their party, regardless of the working-class and peasantry. After the October Revolution – in the context of a developing series of civil conflicts between the nations, religions, regions, classes and political groups of the disintegrating Russian Empire – they began to build this dictatorship."

Cooperate actively in destroying the moral foundations of society and honesty and trust in the government's promises. Infiltrate other parties with your own people, forcing them to vote for what is useful to your own party's interest. "There are no morals in politics; there is only expedience. A scoundrel may be of use to us just because he is a scoundrel." Vladimir Lenin

"The entire purpose of training, educating, and teaching the youth of today should be to imbue them with communist ethics.

But is there such a thing as communist ethics? Is there such a thing as communist morality? Of course, there is. It is often suggested that we have no ethics of our own; very often the bourgeoisie accuse us Communists of rejecting all morality. This is a method of confusing the issue, of throwing dust in the eyes of the workers and peasants.

In what sense do we reject ethics, reject morality?.............. We say that our morality is entirely subordinated to the interests of the proletariat's class struggle. Our morality stems from the interests of the class struggle of the proletariat." V.I. Lenin, "The Tasks of the Youth Leagues"

This is saying that communist ethics and morality is really "the ends justify the means."

It has always been a basic principle of Lenin that his party must be a small group of professional revolutionaries. But to accomplish the goals of this elite group, they cannot and dare not remain in isolation from all of society. Their job is not only to conspire and when necessary to undermine, but it is also to influence and direct the opinions and actions of all the people from workers to the capitalists.

Lenin's understanding of the necessity of this influence predates the Bolshevik Revolution of 1917, as Lenin wrote in his "What Is To Be Done," and elsewhere, began to stress the difference between the functions of the elite group (Party) and those on the outside of this Party, primarily aimed at mass organizations such as trade unions and other political parties. He pointed out that under the indirect hidden control and guidance of the Party, such organizations could attract far greater support than the Party itself could ever hope to get. He wrote about the importance of transmission belts from the Party to the masses. Without these transmission belts, the Party could not hope to maintain itself, much less grow and expand.

Register everyone who has firearms, in order to confiscate them when the time comes, preventing them from opposing your revolution. "An oppressed class which does not strive to learn to use arms, to acquire arms, only deserves to be treated like slaves. We cannot, unless we have become bourgeois pacifists or opportunists, forget that we are living in a class society from which there is no way out, nor can there be, save through the class struggle. In every class society, whether based on slavery, serfdom, or, as at present, wage-labor, the oppressor class is always armed. Not only the modern standing army, but even the modern militia - and even in the most democratic bourgeois republics, Switzerland, for instance - represent the bourgeoisie armed against the proletariat. That is such an elementary truth that it is hardly necessary to dwell upon it. Suffice it to point to the use of troops against strikers in all capitalist countries.

A bourgeoisie armed against the proletariat is one of the biggest fundamental and cardinal facts of modern capitalist society. And in face of this fact, revolutionary Social-Democrats are urged to "demand" "disarmament"! That is tantamount of complete abandonment of the class-struggle point of view, to renunciation of all thought of revolution. Our slogan must be arming of the proletariat to defeat, expropriate and disarm the bourgeoisie. These are the only tactics possible for a revolutionary class, tactics that follow logically from, and are dictated by, the whole objective development of capitalist militarism. Only after the proletariat has disarmed the bourgeoisie will it be able, without betraying its world-historic mission, to consign all armaments to the scrapheap. And the proletariat will undoubtedly do this, but only when this condition has been fulfilled, certainly not before." Vladimir Ilyich Lenin, The Military Program of the Proletarian Revolution

"A system of licensing and registration is the perfect device to deny gun ownership to the bourgeoisie." Vladimir Ilyich Lenin

The Bolshevik Revolution put an end to the free circulation of guns among the general public. The Bolshevik's knew of what the people were capable if they were armed, and moved to strictly control gun ownership. In 1918 the Bolsheviks initiated a large-scale confiscation of civilian firearms, outlawing their possession and threatening up to 10 years in prison for concealing a gun. The only exception was made for hunters who were allowed to possess smoothbore weapons. Gun licenses, however, were still strictly regulated.

I trust, as you were reading through the ten points Lenin knew where critical to his ability to transform a Russian society to a Marxist society, you took note on how these same principles are being championed today in the United States. Those who proclaim these same points are necessary for the good of the United States, also claim they will bring freedom to the people and preserve the American Democracy.

6. COMMUNIST GOALS

On January 10, 1963, the House of Representatives and later the Senate began reviewing a document entitled 'Communist Goals for Taking Over America.' It contained an agenda of 45 separate issues (attacks and techniques) that, in hindsight, were quite shocking then and equally stunning today. Any Congressmen can enter anything into the Congressional Record. This was not a big speech that enraptured Congress. A work like this being cited word for word in the Congressional Record is not that unusual. What is unusual is that somebody found this text was in the Congressional Record and started to spread it on the internet.

THE 45 COMMUNIST GOALS AS READ INTO THE CONGRESSIONAL RECORD, 1963

Congressional Record–Appendix, pp. A34-A35

January 10, 1963

Current Communist Goals

EXTENSION OF REMARKS OF HON. A. S. HERLONG, JR. OF FLORIDA

IN THE HOUSE OF REPRESENTATIVES

Thursday, January 10, 1963

Mr. HERLONG. Mr. Speaker, Mrs. Patricia Nordman of De Land, Fla., is an ardent and articulate opponent of communism, and until recently published the De Land Courier, which she dedicated to the purpose of alerting the public to the dangers of communism in America.

At Mrs. Nordman's request, I include in the RECORD, under unanimous consent, the following "Current Communist Goals," which she identifies as an excerpt from "The Naked Communist," by Cleon Skousen:

1. U.S. acceptance of coexistence as the only alternative to atomic war.

2. U.S. willingness to capitulate in preference to engaging in atomic war.

3. Develop the illusion that total disarmament [by] the United States would be a demonstration of moral strength.

4. Permit free trade between all nations regardless of Communist affiliation and regardless of whether or not items could be used for war.

5. Extension of long-term loans to Russia and Soviet satellites.

6. Provide American aid to all nations regardless of Communist domination.

7. Grant recognition of Red China. Admission of Red China to the U.N.

8. Set up East and West Germany as separate states in spite of Khrushchev's promise in 1955 to settle the German question by free elections under supervision of the U.N.

9. Prolong the conferences to ban atomic tests because the United States has agreed to suspend tests as long as negotiations are in progress.

10. Allow all Soviet satellites individual representation in the U.N.

11. Promote the U.N. as the only hope for mankind. If its charter is rewritten, demand that it be set up as a one-world government with its own independent armed forces. (Some Communist

leaders believe the world can be taken over as easily by the U.N. as by Moscow. Sometimes these two centers compete with each other as they are now doing in the Congo.)

12. Resist any attempt to outlaw the Communist Party.

13. Do away with all loyalty oaths.

14. Continue giving Russia access to the U.S. Patent Office.

15. Capture one or both of the political parties in the United States.

16. Use technical decisions of the courts to weaken basic American institutions by claiming their activities violate civil rights.

17. Get control of the schools. Use them as transmission belts for socialism and current Communist propaganda. Soften the curriculum. Get control of teachers' associations. Put the party line in textbooks.

18. Gain control of all student newspapers.

19. Use student riots to foment public protests against programs or organizations which are under Communist attack.

20. Infiltrate the press. Get control of book-review assignments, editorial writing, policymaking positions.

21. Gain control of key positions in radio, TV, and motion pictures.

22. Continue discrediting American culture by degrading all forms of artistic expression. An American Communist cell was told to "eliminate all good sculpture from parks and buildings, substitute shapeless, awkward and meaningless forms."

23. Control art critics and directors of art museums. "Our plan is to promote ugliness, repulsive, meaningless art."

24. Eliminate all laws governing obscenity by calling them "censorship" and a violation of free speech and free press.

25. Break down cultural standards of morality by promoting pornography and obscenity in books, magazines, motion pictures, radio, and TV.

26. Present homosexuality, degeneracy, and promiscuity as "normal, natural, healthy."

27. Infiltrate the churches and replace revealed religion with "social" religion. Discredit the Bible and emphasize the need for intellectual maturity which does not need a "religious crutch."

28. Eliminate prayer or any phase of religious expression in the schools on the ground that it violates the principle of "separation of church and state."

29. Discredit the American Constitution by calling it inadequate, old-fashioned, out of step with modern needs, a hindrance to cooperation between nations on a worldwide basis.

30. Discredit the American Founding Fathers. Present them as selfish aristocrats who had no concern for the "common man."

31. Belittle all forms of American culture and discourage the teaching of American history on the ground that it was only a minor part of the "big picture." Give more emphasis to Russian history since the Communists took over.

32. Support any socialist movement to give centralized control over any part of the culture—education, social agencies, welfare programs, mental health clinics, etc.

33. Eliminate all laws or procedures which interfere with the operation of the Communist apparatus.

34. Eliminate the House Committee on Un-American Activities.

35. Discredit and eventually dismantle the FBI.

36. Infiltrate and gain control of more unions.

37. Infiltrate and gain control of big business.

38. Transfer some of the powers of arrest from the police to social agencies. Treat all behavioral problems as psychiatric disorders which no one but psychiatrists can understand [or treat].

39. Dominate the psychiatric profession and use mental health laws as a means of gaining coercive control over those who oppose Communist goals.

40. Discredit the family as an institution. Encourage promiscuity and easy divorce.

41. Emphasize the need to raise children away from the negative influence of parents. Attribute prejudices, mental blocks, and retarding of children to suppressive influence of parents.

42. Create the impression that violence and insurrection are legitimate aspects of the American tradition; that students and special-interest groups should rise up and use ["] united force ["] to solve economic, political, or social problems.

43. Overthrow all colonial governments before native populations are ready for self-government.

44. Internationalize the Panama Canal.

45. Repeal the Connally reservation so the United States cannot prevent the World Court

End of entry.

All of these goals have been addressed in one way or another. Many of them were applicable specifically to the relationship between the United States and he Soviet Union and its communist allies prior to the end of the cold war. What I will do is concentrate on those points that apply to the transformation of the United States culturally, that same transformation to which the Obama's referred in their calls to transform the United States.

3. Develop the illusion that total disarmament [by] the United States would be a demonstration of moral strength. Those who have advocated for a nuclear freeze supported a freeze on American nuclear development only. Rarely were Soviet nukes or those of other nations mentioned with the notable exception of Ronald Reagan. The same advocates still call for reducing American military might, stating that there is something immoral about America preserving its military pre-eminence in the world. Obama said, "A world without nuclear weapons is profoundly in America's interest and the world's interest. It is our responsibility to make the commitment, and to do the hard work to make this vision a reality."

4. Permit free trade between all nations regardless of Communist affiliation and regardless of whether or not items could be used for war. Despite a cyber-warfare truce, a defense analyst said China is probably still engaged in the theft of sensitive U.S. military technology. Hacking over the years is one of the reasons China has been able to narrow the gap with the United States in advanced missiles, drone technology and even stealth aircraft. It is a known fact that China openly steels American technology for defense and other purposes.

7. Grant recognition of Red China. Admission of Red China to the U.N. On Oct. 25, 1971, the United Nations General Assembly voted to admit the People's Republic of China (mainland China) and to expel the Republic of China (Taiwan). The Communist P.R.C. therefore assumed the R.O.C.'s place in the General Assembly as well as its place as one of the five permanent members of the U.N. Security Council. The United States did oppose this resolution.

11. Promote the U.N. as the only hope for mankind. If its charter is rewritten, demand that it be set up as a one-world government with its own independent armed forces. (Some Communist leaders believe the world can be taken over as easily by the U.N. as by Moscow. Sometimes these two centers compete with each other as they are now doing in the Congo.) In his final speech to the United Nations Security Council, Barack Obama said the United States has to give up some freedom in exchange for security. "We can only realize the promise of this institution's founding to replace the ravages of war with cooperation if powerful nations, like my own, accept constraints," Obama said.

"Sometimes I am criticized in my country for professing a belief in international norms and multilateral institutions, but I am convinced in the long run, giving up some freedom of action, not giving up our ability to protect ourselves or pursue our core interests, but binding ourselves to the international rules over the long-term enhances our security," Obama concluded.

12. Resist any attempt to outlaw the Communist Party. According to Wikipedia, the Communist Control Act (68 Stat. 775, 50 U.S.C. 841-844) is a piece of United States federal legislation, signed into law by President Dwight Eisenhower on August 24, 1954, which outlaws the Communist Party of the United States and criminalizes membership in, or support for the Party or "Communist-action" organizations and defines evidence to be considered by a jury in determining participation in the activities, planning, actions, objectives, or purposes of such organizations.

In California, a bill to end a decades-old ban on members of the Communist Party working in its government, was introduced. The bill's sponsor, Assemblyman Rob Bonta, said that California's laws should focus on individuals' actions and evidence rather than political affiliations and what he termed "empty labels." He called his legislation a "cleanup bill that removes archaic and outdated references to the Communist Party in our state laws, specifically those stating that a public employee may be dismissed from employment if he or she advocates or is knowingly a member of the Communist Party."

The bill passed in a 41-30 vote, after a debate that touched on the Cold War, the U.S. history of fighting communism — and the potential for future conflicts. It was later dropped.

13. Do away with all loyalty oaths. On June 1, 1964, the United States Supreme Court struck down Washington laws requiring state employees to take loyalty oaths. In 1951, the state of

Washington Legislature imposed a loyalty oath requirement for all state employees. In 1955, the statute was amended to require employees to swear that "I am not a subversive person." According to the law, a "subversive person" was:

"any person who commits, attempts to commit, or aids in the commission, or advocates, abets, advises or teaches by any means any person to commit, attempt to commit, or aid in the commission of any act intended to overthrow, destroy or alter, or to assist in the overthrow, destruction or alteration of, the constitutional form of the government of the United States, or of the state of Washington, or any political subdivision of either of them by revolution, force, or violence; or who with knowledge ... becomes or remains a member of a subversive organization."

"Subversive organization" was defined in the same terms used in the definition of subversive person, and the law also specifically declared the Communist Party a subversive organization.

The Court held that "the oath requirements and the statutory provisions on which they are based are invalid on their face because their language is unduly vague, uncertain, and broad."

Remember, this was the Warren Court.

15. Capture one or both of the political parties in the United States. Norman Thomas, six-time Presidential Candidate for the Socialist Party of America, in a 1944 speech said, "The American people will never knowingly adopt Socialism. But, under the name of 'Liberalism', they will adopt every fragment of the Socialist program until one day America will be a Socialist nation, without knowing how it happened."

He went on to say: "I no longer need to run as a Presidential Candidate for the Socialist Party. The Democrat Party has adopted our platform."

As of today, the Democrat Party is now advocating for the same policies outlined by Karl Marx and implemented by Lenin, Hitler, Mao, Castro, and Chavez. There is no discernable difference between the Communist Party and the Democrat Party; check the lists of the Communist Manifesto and the policies implemented by Lenin.

16. Use technical decisions of the courts to weaken basic American institutions by claiming their activities violate civil rights. The American Civil Liberties Union (ACLU) was founded in 1920 by Roger Baldwin, Crystal Eastman, and others. The stated goal of the ACLU is to "defend and preserve the individual rights and liberties guaranteed to every person by the Bill of Rights of the U.S. Constitution and laws of the United States." It has however fought to use technical decisions of the courts to weaken American liberties and values.

"I am for socialism, disarmament, and ultimately for abolishing the state itself as an instrument of violence and compulsion. I seek the social ownership of property, the abolition of the propertied class and sole control by those who produce wealth. Communism is, of course, the goal." ACLU founder Roger Baldwin, 1935

Some ACLU cases:

1931 Stromberg v. California

The ACLU argued successfully that the conviction of a communist for displaying a red flag should be overturned because it was based on a state law that was overly vague, in violation of the First Amendment.

1937 DeJonge v. Oregon

A landmark First Amendment case, in which the Court held that the defendant's conviction under a state criminal syndicalism statute merely for attending a peaceful Communist Party rally violated his free speech rights.

1957 Watkins v. United States

Under the First Amendment, the Court imposed limits on the investigative powers of the House Un-American Activities Committee, which had found a labor leader in contempt for refusing to answer questions about his associates' membership in the Communist Party.

1958 Kent v. Dulles

The Court ruled that the State Department had exceeded its authority in denying artist Rockwell Kent a passport because he refused to sign a "noncommunist affidavit." The right to travel, said the Court, is protected by the Due Process Clause of the Fifth Amendment.

1964 Jacobellis v. Ohio

Justice Potter Stewart's famous statement that, although he could not define "obscenity," he "knew it when he saw it," crowned the Court's overturning of a cinema owner's conviction for showing "The Lovers," by Louis Malle.

1971 Cohen v. California

Reversed the conviction of a man who allegedly disturbed the peace by wearing a jacket that bore the words, "F__k the draft," while walking through a courthouse corridor. The Court rejected the notion that the state can prohibit speech just because it is "offensive."

1989 Texas v. Johnson

This First Amendment invalidation of the Texas flag desecration statute provoked the newly inaugurated George Bush to propose a federal ban on flag burning or mutilation. Congress swiftly obliged, but the Court struck down the law a year later in United States v. Eichman — in which the ACLU also filed a brief. Both rulings were big victories for symbolic political speech.

1992 Lee v. Weisman

The Court ruled that any officially sanctioned prayer at public school graduation ceremonies violates the Establishment Clause.

17. Get control of the schools. Use them as transmission belts for socialism and current Communist propaganda. Soften the curriculum. Get control of teachers' associations. Put the party line in textbooks. This is from my book "The Road to Tyranny." "Many leaders of the Teachers Union like Jeff Bale and Sarah Knopp, openly state that Marxism must be taught in our schools, that teaching social justice and multiculturalism is essential.

Bale and Knopp co-edited a book entitled 'Education and Capitalism and Learning and Liberation.' This is a book of different articles written by different people in education. All of them sing the praises of Karl Marx, Friedrich Engels, Lev Vygotsky, and many other self-proclaimed collectivists. Every individualist who is concerned about the direction our education system is taking, should read this book. The why our education system is being transformed into a collectivist indoctrination system is made obvious.

In the forward of this book, Bill Bigelow was asked a question and his answer is very revealing. Bill Bigelow taught high school social studies in Portland, Oregon for almost 30 years. He is the curriculum editor of 'Rethinking Schools' and the co-director of the 'Zinn Education Project.' This project offers free materials to teach a fuller 'people's history.'

The question to Bigelow was, 'That same introduction to 'Rethinking our Classrooms' also proclaims, 'classrooms can be places of hope, where student and teacher gain glimpses of the kind of society we could live in and where students learn the academic and critical skills needed to make it a reality.' Can you give a few examples from your experience as a teacher of lessons where you have been able to glimpse this more hopeful society?'

Bigelow answered, 'I've been in a number of social justice curriculum groups over the years, and this is the key conundrum that we always return to: how can we teach fully and honestly about the enormity of injustice in the world and yet not totally discourage students? I think that 'hope' begins with students' experiences in the classroom. It seems to me that when students feel themselves changing and growing-which is fundamental to believing in the possibility of a different kind of society. One simple example is giving students a chance to write about their lives and share their stories with one another-encouraging them to offer each other positive feedback and to ask big questions about how our personal stories connect to broader social patterns.

We also need to give students the opportunity to feel themselves as 'activists'-broadly understood. So, for example, when we study about global sweatshops and the exploitation of poor countries and communities around the world, we do not just leave our students with the memory of 'people being treated badly.' We highlight the resistance of workers in the Global South, who themselves are fighting for dignity. It is important that our students realize that people are already fighting for better lives, and our role is simply to do our part in the solidarity.

Role plays can reinforce this, too-putting students in the position of organizers; Industrial Workers of the World members during the 1912 Bread and Roses strike in Lawrence, Massachusetts; student activists in apartheid South Africa, confronting what they called their 'gutter education;" student environmental justice activists today working around climate change issues.

As a component of the global sweatshops' unit, I assign students 'making a difference' projects to take their learning outside the classroom in order to attempt to make the world a better place. Students have been amazingly creative-they've written children's books that they've read at middle and elementary schools, they've published poetry in community newspapers, they've made raps and videos broadcast on community stations, they've written letters to policy makers, they've organized educations forums for other students. The point is that as teachers we need to pair our teaching of injustice. Hope comes from being part of the solution, to paraphrase a Black Panther maxim. And hope comes from recognizing that they are not alone; that there are people around the world combating despair with activism."

Bigelow defined that these situations are problems and the assignment was to accept that definition and proceed from that point. That is indoctrination. Education would be to have the students research the situation, determine if a problem existed, and if so, define the problem and devise a solution. That would be education.

20. Infiltrate the press. Get control of book-review assignments, editorial writing, policymaking positions. 21. Gain control of key positions in radio, TV, and motion pictures. Ken Stern, former NPR CEO stated, "Most reporters and editors are liberal — a now-dated Pew Research Center poll found that liberals outnumber conservatives in the media by some 5 to 1, and that comports with my own anecdotal experience at National Public Radio. When you are liberal, and everyone else around you are as well, it is easy to fall into groupthink on what stories are important, what sources are legitimate and what the narrative of the day will be."

24. Eliminate all laws governing obscenity by calling them "censorship" and a violation of free speech and free press. 25. Break down cultural

standards of morality by promoting pornography and obscenity in books, magazines, motion pictures, radio, and TV. Today, pornography and obscenity are available through increasingly sexually explicit movies and television programs, magazines, video tapes, and most recently, the Internet. The Internet brings pornography into our homes, schools, and libraries. Everything from soft-core to hard-core to child pornography is now available not just for adults, but for children. Anybody living in the United States is aware or this.

26. Present homosexuality, degeneracy, and promiscuity as "normal, natural, healthy." The Democrat Party Platform now includes abortion and same sex 'marriage,' while excluding God. The Democrat Party's platform, formally adopted at the Democratic National Convention in Charlotte, N.C., supports "marriage equality," a phrase used by those who wish to redefine marriage to include homosexual couples. It also agreed with the redefinition of the word "family" in immigration regulations to include homosexual relationships. Affirming its support of abortion with no restrictions, a redefinition of marriage, and free birth control for all women, the Democrat Party said in its official statement of positions that it is committed to "pursuing policies that truly value families." The Democrat platform also removed references to "God." Insisting that "gay rights are human rights," the party also said that the State Department is currently "funding a program that finances gay-rights organizations" and vowed to "actively combat" the actions of other nations that it believes are engaged in "discrimination."

27. Infiltrate the churches and replace revealed religion with "social" religion. Discredit the Bible and emphasize the need for intellectual maturity which does not need a "religious crutch." This is a statement from the National Council of Churches. It reads like it could have come from the writings of Marx and Engels except for the reference to Jesus.

"In the love incarnate in Jesus, despite the world's sufferings and evils, we honor the deep connections within our human family and seek to awaken a new spirit of community, by working for:

• Abatement of hunger and poverty, and enactment of policies benefiting the most vulnerable.

• High-quality public education for all and universal, affordable, and accessible healthcare.

• An effective program of social security during sickness, disability, and old age.

• Tax and budget policies that reduce disparities between rich and poor, strengthen democracy, and provide greater opportunity for everyone within the common good.

• Just immigration policies that protect family unity, safeguard workers' rights, require employer accountability, and foster international cooperation.

• Sustainable communities marked by affordable housing, access to good jobs, and public safety.

• Public service as a high vocation, with real limits on the power of private interests in politics.

In hope sustained by the Holy Spirit, we pledge to be peacemakers in the world and stewards of God's good creation, by working for:

• Adoption of simpler lifestyles for those who have enough; grace over greed in economic life.

• Access for all to clean air and water and healthy food, through wise care of land and technology.

• Sustainable use of earth's resources, promoting alternative energy sources and public transportation with binding covenants to reduce global warming and protect populations most affected.

• Equitable global trade and aid that protects local economies, cultures, and livelihoods.

• Peacemaking through multilateral diplomacy rather than unilateral force, the abolition of torture, and a strengthening of the United Nations and the rule of international law.

• Nuclear disarmament and redirection of military spending to more peaceful and productive uses.

• Cooperation and dialogue for peace and environmental justice among the world's religions.

28. Eliminate prayer or any phase of religious expression in the schools on the ground that it violates the principle of "separation of church and state." Facts and case summary for Engel v. Vitale,

370 U.S. 421 (1962) School-sponsored prayer in public schools is unconstitutional.

A New York State law required public schools to open each day with the Pledge of Allegiance and a nondenominational prayer in which the students recognized their dependence upon God. The law allowed students to absent themselves from this activity if they found it objectionable. A parent sued on behalf of his child, arguing that the law violated the Establishment Clause of the First Amendment, as made applicable to the states through the Due Process Clause of the Fourteenth Amendment.

The majority, via Justice Black, held that school-sponsored prayer violates the Establishment Clause of the First Amendment. The majority stated that the provision allowing students to absent themselves from this activity did not make the law constitutional because the purpose of the First Amendment was to prevent government interference with religion. The majority noted that religion is especially important to a vast majority of the American people. Since Americans adhere to a wide variety of beliefs, it is not appropriate for the government to endorse any particular belief system. The majority noted that wars, persecutions, and other destructive measures often arose in the past when the government involved itself in religious affairs.

In his concurrence, Justice Douglas took an even broader view of the Establishment Clause, arguing that any type of public promotion of religion, including giving financial aid to religious schools, violates the Establishment Clause.

29. Discredit the American Constitution by calling it inadequate, old-fashioned, out of step with modern needs, a hindrance to cooperation between nations on a worldwide basis. 30. Discredit the American Founding Fathers. Present them as selfish aristocrats who had no concern for the "common man." These are excerpts from an article by Galanty Miller in 2014 entitled "The Constitution Is Outdated; Let's Change It."

For years, society ignored the founding fathers' association with slavery. But things changed. And now we are constantly reminded that these rich white men were slave owners. But we have become emotionally detached from the words. To say "slave owner" does not carry much of an impact. We do not describe these men as being evil and despicable, and they auctioned off children and raped little girls and they forced human beings to spend all day, every day, out in the hot fields to do physically exhausting, mind-numbing work.

The Constitution was written by very flawed men, who owned human beings, whose foresight has been proven inaccurate, and who prayed to dogs. Americans today should not take every word of it as the gospel. (Note: Though I think I might have read about the "praying to dogs" thing in a dream.)

The Constitution is a political blueprint for a time when white people owned black people, the average life span was 35 years old, and news was spread through people yelling on the street. Today, white people marry black people and news is spread through people yelling on cable channels. Things have changed."

On September 6, 2001 Barack Obama called the United States Constitution "a deeply flawed document."

An op-ed piece in the New York Times by Meagan Day and Bhaskar Sunkara states, "The Byzantine Constitution that [James Madison] helped create serves as the foundation for a system of government that rules over people, rather than an evolving tool for popular self-government." They go on to write, "As long as we think of our Constitution as a sacred document, instead of an outdated relic, we'll have to deal with its anti-democratic consequences."

40. Discredit the family as an institution. Encourage promiscuity and easy divorce. 41. Emphasize the need to raise children away from the negative influence of parents. Attribute prejudices, mental blocks, and retarding of children to suppressive influence of parents. This is a mandatory requirement of any Communist movement. We find it reiterated throughout the writings of Marx and Lenin. It is a major part of any Communist takeover. A society with a strong family unit is a society that is not easy to control. The communist movement requires a conforming or totally indoctrinated people. When strong family units exist, the society is a society of varied ideas and values. The children are more likely to question the demands typically made of a communist government; thus, the likelihood of dissent is much greater.

Communists believe the child is a ward of the state and that it is the responsibility of the state to teach or indoctrinate all children with communist, collectivist, and conforming values. Marx said the child should be removed from the mother as soon as the child can be nourished when away from the mother. The communists have also found this requirement to be necessary because it becomes easier to remove God from the society and make the society an immoral and Godless society.

44. Internationalize the Panama Canal. On September 7, 1977, President Jimmy Carter signed the Panama Canal Treaty and Neutrality Treaty promising to give control of the canal to the Panamanians by the year 2000.

45. Repeal the Connally reservation. This is so the United States cannot prevent the World Court from seizing jurisdiction over domestic problems. A repeal would give the World Court jurisdiction over United States domestic problems. The repeal would not only give the World Court jurisdiction over our nation, but also individuals, you, and me.

The Connally Reservation was set up to keep The World Court (United Nations) from interfering with American matters on things such as tariffs, immigration laws, school curriculums, gun control, etc. Many times, the United Nations has tried to say, that such things were "foreign" and not "domestic" and therefore would fall under the United Nations jurisdiction. It is this Connally Reservation, that states that America will decide what is its business and what is the world's business. It is that law, that "legally" protects us from being taken over by the United Nations.

By reviewing these 45 goals of how the communists would transform the United States, you can see that at the very least, progress has been made on all of them. Many of these 45 goals are now accepted and referred to as the "American Way." The transformation is alive and well. Our goal, you, who are concerned enough about the United States not succumbing to this transformation by taking the time and making the effort to learn, and me, must be to alert as many

Americans as we can to this transformation of the United States, from a free and independent nation and people, to a Marxist totalitarian state under the domination of the "Dictatorship of the Proletariat". A transformation that you can see, is well under way.

7. A SPECTRE IS HAUNTING AMERICA

A spectre is haunting the United States and that spectre is collectivism.

A spectre is a spirit, especially one of a terrifying nature. It is a source of terror or dread. Collectivism is the practice or principle of giving the group priority over each individual in it. The rights, ambitions, and liberties of any individual are always subordinated to that of the group. If it is determined that the individual in any way threatens what is determined to be the good of the group, the individual must conform to the dictates of the group or the individual is segregated from the group into a place of isolation or eliminated completely. Collectivism is an all-encompassing term that includes Marxism, communism, socialism, progressive, and todays Democrats. These are all virtually the same. There are minor differences, but collectivism ultimately leads to what Marx called his classless society that would be totally conforming and totally equal.

The fundamental political conflict in America today is, as it has been for a century, individualism vs. collectivism. Does the individual's life belong to him—or does it belong to the group, the community, society, or the state? With government expanding ever more rapidly—seizing and spending more and more of our money on "entitlement" programs and corporate bailouts, and intruding on our businesses and lives in increasingly onerous ways—the need for clarity on this issue has never been greater.

Individualism is the idea that the individual's life belongs to him and that he has an inalienable right to live it as he sees fit, to act on his own judgment, to keep and use the product of his effort, and to pursue the values of his choosing. It is the idea that the individual is sovereign, an end to himself, and the fundamental unit of moral concern. This is the ideal that the American Founders set forth and sought to establish when they drafted and adopted the Declaration of Independence and the Constitution of the United States. They formed a country in which the individual's natural rights to life, liberty, property, and the pursuit of happiness were to be accepted as being endowed by the Creator and protected as such.

Collectivism is the idea that the individual's life belongs not to him but to the group or society of which he is merely a part, that the individual has no rights, and that the individual must sacrifice their values and goals for the group's "greater good," as defined by the group. According to collectivism, the group or society is the basic unit of moral concern, and the individual is of value only insofar as they serve the group. As one advocate of this idea puts it: "Man has no rights except those which society permits him to enjoy. From the day of his birth until the day of his death, society allows him to enjoy certain so-called rights and deprives him of others; not . . . because society desires especially to favor or oppress the individual, but because its own preservation, welfare, and happiness are the prime considerations."

The United States was purposefully founded as a country based on individualism as opposed to collectivism. Republics are types of government that protect the individual rights of each individual. Democracies are forms of government that demand the individual forfeit their rights when they do not conform to the majority. Free enterprise economies or capitalism is associated with individualism where each individual is rewarded for their efforts and production. Economies controlled by central planning committees or government, are associated with collectivism, which is again an all-encompassing term for Marxism, communism, socialism, progressive, and todays Democrat.

A few common characteristics of individualist cultures include:

Individual rights take center stage – the Bill of Rights

Independence is highly valued

Being dependent upon others is often considered shameful or embarrassing

People tend to be self-reliant

People who are deemed to be successful, overachievers, and innovators are respected and highly regarded

People place a greater emphasis on standing out and being unique – non-conformity

Being dependent upon others is often considered shameful or embarrassing – people try to get off welfare as quickly as possible

People tend to be achievers, entrepreneurs, hard workers, take pride in providing for family

The rights of individuals tend to take a high precedence

People tend to accept the consequences of their decisions – if the consequences happen to be bad, they learn from them, move on, and try again

A few common characteristics of collectivist cultures include:

In a collectivist society the needs of the community are placed above the ambition of the individual

Conformity is stressed. Non-conformity is at best frowned upon and at worst punished

Equality, especially economic equality, is stressed

Successful and ambitious individuals are demonized, ostracized, and many times segregated or even eliminated

Individual rights, such as speech, are limited to speech that is defined as politically correct or acceptable

Collectivism is identified with government control over economies, socialism, and over individual behavior and thoughts, communism

Government reliance is accepted and promoted for healthy and capable people, to be a ward of the state carries no negative consequences

Society is held responsible for bad decisions of the individual and the state is expected to make a person whole if they suffer financial loss

When we are told that the United States will be fundamentally transformed, the logical question would be, transformed from what to what. The United States was formed and based on the concept that natural rights are given to each individual from the Creator and that the only role government had over natural rights was to protect those natural rights for each individual. We were also formed as a republic and not a democracy and as an individualist society and not a collectivist society.

What would the role of government be in this unique and special nation that was formed as no other nation had ever been formed. When Samuel Adams said in November of 1772, that the colonists were given the natural rights of life, liberty, and property; and when Thomas Jefferson wrote in the Declaration of Independence that "we are endowed by our Creator with certain unalienable rights, and amongst them are life, liberty, and the pursuit of happiness," they were writing based on what they had learned from the great philosopher John Locke.

John Locke also said the role of government should be limited to securing the life and property of its citizens, and is only necessary because in an ideal, anarchic state of nature, various problems arise that would make life more insecure than under the protection of a minimal state.

This was also the intent of the founding fathers. They understood that freedom and liberty could only prevail and prosper when the government was limited. Every power given to or assumed by government was a limitation on the freedom and liberty of the individual. Consequently, our Constitution established specific powers for the federal government, powers that are limited and enumerated. The founders believed that the government exists to perform only those services that the people cannot provide for themselves, such as national defense.

James Madison told us, "If Congress can employ money indefinitely, for the general welfare, and are the sole and supreme judges of the general welfare, they may take the care of religion into their own hands; they may appoint teachers in every state, county, and parish, and pay them out of the public treasury; they may take into their own hands the education of children, the establishing in like manner schools throughout the union; they may assume the provision of the poor.... Were the power of Congress to be established in the latitude contended for, it would subvert the very foundations, and transmute the very nature of the limited government established by the people of America."

From the Federalist Papers we are told, "The purpose of the United States Constitution is to limit the power of the federal government, not the American people."

Thomas Jefferson explained, "A wise and frugal government, leave men free to regulate their own pursuits of industry and improvement, and shall not take from their mouth of labor the bread it has earned – this is the sum of good government."

From Thomas Paine, "Government, even in its best state, is but a necessary evil; in its worst state, an intolerable one."

What is this spectre of collectivism that is haunting the United States, this terrifying spirit or ghost? It is that period of time that Marx told us will follow the time of capitalism, or the transition time between capitalism and communism. This is as Lenin said, "the time of socialism which is the gateway to communism." Marx explained that during this time period the proletariat would be in total command implementing the necessary policies to compete the transition. Government and society would be under the total control of the proletariat, the majority, or as Marx stated the "Dictatorship of the Proletariat."

Marx went on to explain that the proletariat must be forceful in their advancement and that despotic means would be necessary and acceptable. In all transitions, Russia, Eastern Europe, Germany, China, Cuba, and Venezuela to name a few, we have learned that despotic means has no limits so long as the desired end is achieved. The axiom "The ends always justify the means," is real and is not applied gently or sparingly.

"No Marxist can deny that the interests of socialism are higher than the interests of the right of nations to self-determination," said Lenin. "The role of government is to implement socialism."

Lenin went on to explain what limits should be placed on government when he said, "Dictatorship is rule based directly upon force and unrestricted by any laws. The revolutionary dictatorship of the proletariat is rule won and maintained by the use of violence by the proletariat against the bourgeoisie, rule that is unrestricted by any laws."

And just what is the extent of that violence government must use to gain and keep control was explained by Lenin when he demanded, "Comrades! The kulak uprising in your five districts must be crushed without pity. You must make example of these people. (1) Hang (I mean hang publicly, so that people see it) at least 100 kulaks, rich bastards, and known bloodsuckers. (2) Publish their names. (3) Seize all their grain. (4) Single out the hostages per my instructions in yesterday's telegram. Do all this so that for miles around people see it all, understand it, tremble, and tell themselves that we are killing the bloodthirsty kulaks and that we will continue to do so ...Find tougher people. "

Franklin Roosevelt explained his philosophy of government expansion and control when he said, "Men may differ as to the particular form of governmental activity with respect to industry and business, but nearly all men are agreed that private enterprise in times such as these cannot be left without assistance and without reasonable safeguards lest it destroy not only itself but also our processes of civilization."

And FDR sang the glories of the Marx required steeply progressive income tax when he said, "Taxation according to income is the most effective instrument yet devised to obtain just contribution from those best able to bear it and to avoid placing onerous burdens upon the mass of our people." Notice how the phrasing used by FDR is the same phrasing used by collectivists always, including those of today.

Barack Obama told a group of students that they should not believe those who tell them they should fear government, but that government was their friend.

The views of government held by individualists and collectivists are exactly the opposite. The individualist believes as government gains power, the people lose freedom and liberty. The individualist believes that their freedom lies in their ability to make their own decisions, to live their own life, and to have their own thoughts.

The collectivist believes that the people are free when they have been relieved from the burden of making their own decisions, living their own life, and having their own thoughts. Under collectivism the individual is free from those obligations and is not responsible for any consequences. The person is expected to and learns to depend on the state.

In 1830, a young judge from France arrived in America. His name was Alexis de Tocqueville. He came to study the American system. He and his friend soaked up more information about the great American experiment in ten months than most scholars absorb in a lifetime. Returning to France, Alexis de Tocqueville wrote a two-volume work entitled, "Democracy in America." De Tocqueville saw the people of the United States passing through several distinct stages. First of all, he saw the strength of character and moral integrity that would make them prosperous. But as they became self-sufficient, he saw that they would be less concerned about each other and much less concerned about the principles that made them a great people. This would leave them vulnerable to the manipulation of clever politicians who would begin to promise them perpetual security if they accepted certain schemes contrived by some of their leaders. He then described what modern students have been led to identify as "democratic socialism.": "That power is absolute, minute, regular, provident, and mild. It would be like the authority of a parent, if, like that authority, its object was to prepare men for manhood; but it seeks on the contrary to keep them in perpetual childhood; it is well content that the people should rejoice, provided they think of nothing but rejoicing. "For their happiness such a government willingly labors, but it chooses to be the sole agent and the only arbiter of that happiness; it provides for their security, foresees and supplies their necessities, facilitates their pleasures, manages their principal concerns, directs their industry, regulates the descent of property, and subdivides their inheritances -- what remains, to spare them all the care of thinking and the trouble of living." "After having thus successively taken each member of the community in its powerful grasp, and fashioned them at will, the supreme power then extends its arm over the whole community. It covers the surface of society with a network of small complicated rules, minute, and uniform, through which the most original minds and the most energetic characters cannot penetrate, to rise above the crowd. "The will of man is not shattered, but softened, bent, and guided -- men are seldom forced by it to act, but they are constantly restrained from acting. Such a power does not destroy, but it prevents existence; it does not tyrannize, but it compresses, enervates, extinguishes, and stupefies a people, till [the] nation is reduced to be nothing better than a flock of timid and industrious animals, of which the government is the shepherd." (From the National Center for Constitutional Studies - The Warnings of Alex De Tocqueville)

Alex De Tocqueville described the fundamental transformation that was promised by Barack Obama, that same transformation championed by those such as Marx and Lenin, and the same transformation that is underway in the United States today. It is being called on to continue until the people are a "flock of timid and industrious animals, of which the government is the shepherd." This is not what our founders intended and what they purposefully tried to prevent by designing our nation so that we would always have a limited government with a dynamic and sovereign people striving to fulfill their individual dreams, unhindered by the collectivist constraints of government.

8. FATHER OF THE AMERICAN REVOLUTION

The father of the American Revolution – Samuel Adams

"It does not take a majority to prevail but an irate tireless minority keen on setting brushfires of freedom in the minds of men." Samuel Adams

George Washington is known as the Father of our Country. Thomas Jefferson is known as the author of the Declaration of Independence. John Adams is often times, and rightfully so, recognized as his assistant author. James Madison is often referred to as the author of, or certainly the force behind, the United States Constitution and the Bill of Rights. Alexander Hamilton, along with James Madison, and to a lesser extent John Jay authored the Federalist Papers. All great patriots and amongst those known as the Founding Fathers.

I would make the argument that George Washington, Thomas Jefferson, John Adams, James Madison, Alexander Hamilton, John Jay, or any of the other great American patriots, Founding Fathers, and revolutionaries would not be in history books, or if they were it would be as very minor figures, if it were not for **Samuel Adams, The Father of the American Revolution.**

Other than John Jay, who helped negotiate the Treaty of Paris of 1783, along with Benjamin Franklin and John Adams, and was the first Chief Justice of the Supreme Court, Samuel Adams is perhaps the least known. After Samuel Adams signed the Declaration of Independence, and served in the Continental Congress for a number of years, he went back to Boston and Massachusetts politics. He became much less involved in national affairs. The Declaration of Independence, or the Colonies declaring their independence from Great Britain, the King, and Parliament was the foremost goal of Samuel Adams. There were times when it seemed Samuel Adams was the only person in the colonies with independence as their goal, especially during that time period between later 1770 to mid to late 1773, often times referred to as the quiet time.

Even during this period, when the other notable Whigs had temporized their revolutionary spirits and settled into a routine of tranquility, Samuel

Adams continued to write and organize, constantly reminding the people of Boston, Massachusetts and the Americans in other colonies, that their freedoms and liberties were in constant danger of being removed by the tyrants in London. It was during this time period that Samuel Adams was able to form and organize the committees of correspondence network of Massachusetts that became the prototype for the committees of correspondence for the colonies.

A quick review of the different Acts, and actions taken by the British, along with the response to those Acts and actions by the colonists, would help us understand how Samuel Adams was able to continue to fan that flame of resistance that became the flame of rebellion. Samuel Adams never believed or sought resistance that would lead to a harmonious relationship between Great Britain and the colonies. His purpose, you might say obsession, was complete separation and independence from the King and Parliament.

Samuel Adams became incensed when the British Parliament passed the Sugar Act of 1764. The Sugar Act, also known as the American Revenue Act, was a revenue-raising act passed by Parliament in April 1764. The earlier Molasses Act of 1733, which had imposed a tax of six pence per gallon of molasses, had never been effectively collected due to colonial resistance and evasion. The Sugar Act reduced the rate to be collected by half, but implemented measures to more effectively enforce the tax. The British intended that the new tax on sugar would actually be collected.

Adams took the position that the British Parliament had no authority to tax the American colonists because the colonists were not represented in the Parliament – no taxation without representation. Adams also suggested that all of Massachusetts should present a united front against the Sugar Act. When the Boston Town Meeting approved Samuel Adams instructions on May 24, 1764, it became the first political body in the colonies to state that Parliament could not tax the colonists. By mid-1765 the colonial merchants were calling for a boycott of British goods in retaliation for the Sugar Act.

The Stamp Act of 1765 was the first internal tax levied directly on American colonists by Parliament. This act imposed a tax on all paper documents in the colonies. Samuel Adams led the argument that only their own representative assemblies, those in Massachusetts, could tax Massachusetts citizens, and thus the Stamp Act was unconstitutional. The very nature of the Stamp Act required that stamp collectors be involved on behalf of the Parliament. The colonists resorted to mob violence to intimidate stamp collectors into resigning. The Stamp Act was repealed in 1766, but Parliament issued a Declaratory Act at the same time to reaffirm that Parliament had authority to pass any colonial legislation it saw fit.

The Townshend Acts or Duties of 1767 imposed duties on British china, glass, lead, paint, paper, and tea imported to the colonies. Benjamin Franklin, who was the agent for the Pennsylvania Assembly in London at the time, had informed the British Parliament that the colonies intended to start manufacturing their own goods rather than paying duties on imports. The particular items in the Townshend Acts were chosen for taxation because Charles Townshend, the British Chancellor of the Exchequer, thought these items would be difficult things for the colonists to produce on their own. He estimated the duties would raise approximately 40,000 pounds, with most of the revenue coming from tea.

While the original intent of the import duties had been to raise revenue, Townshend saw the policies as a way to remodel colonial governments. The Townshend Acts would use the revenue raised by the duties to pay the salaries of colonial governors and judges, ensuring the loyalty of America's governmental officials to the British Crown. This would become a major issue that Samuel Adams used to rally the colonists during the quiet time.

A boycott of British imports was the result of the "Massachusetts Circular Letter," a statement written by Samuel Adams and James Otis Jr. and passed by the Massachusetts House of Representatives to other colonial legislatures. With the exception of necessities, such as fishing hooks and wire, New England merchants agreed not to import British goods for one year. New York followed suit in April, with an even more restrictive non-importation agreement.

In response to protests and boycotts, the British sent troops to occupy Boston and quell the unrest. By 1769, more than 2,000 British troops had arrived in Boston to "restore order"—a large number considering only about 16,000 people lived in Boston at the time. Skirmishes between patriot colonists and British soldiers became increasingly common. To protest taxes, patriots would vandalize stores and sell the British goods. Tensions between the colonists and British troops finally came to a head on March 5, 1770, when British soldiers shot into an angry mob, killing five American colonists in an event that became known as the "Boston Massacre."

Little did the colonists or British soldiers know that across the ocean on the same day as the Boston Massacre, the Prime Minister of Great Britain, Lord North, had asked Parliament to repeal the Townshend Acts. All of the Townshend Acts— except for the tax on tea—were repealed in April 1770.

We then entered that time period known as the quiet times. During these years, the flames became much more difficult for Samuel Adams to fan. Even his cousin John Adams, spent his time in Braintree, at his home which was 15 miles south of Boston. There he concentrated on his law practice and farming. During this time, a wedge came between Samuel Adams and John Hancock, especially after Hancock accepted a position offered to him by the governor. Others of those who had strongly supported Samuel Adams in his quest for independence, also became complacent.

In 1772, Samuel Adams started to write about the governor and judges who were now being paid by the King and not the citizens of Massachusetts, per the Townsend Acts. When Adams explained what a danger this was to the people of Massachusetts, in that the loyalty of the governor and judges would now be to the King and not to the people of Massachusetts, Samuel Adams quest for independence began to again attract some attention.

The British came to the assistance of Samuel Adams and his movement for independence when on May 10, 1773, they passed the Tea Act. The act was passed to help the British East India Company avoid bankruptcy by giving the company a monopoly on the American Colonies tea market. Because of other taxes being reduced by Parliament to the British East India Company, the cost of tea to the colonists would be reduced, even though the tax of the Townshend Act would remain. Samuel Adams saw this as a means by which the Parliament would not only be able to dictate from whom the colonists must purchase their tea, but it would also implicitly acknowledge that Parliament had a legal right to tax the colonists.

After much back and forth, all would come to a head when the duty on the tea in the Boston Harbor became due on December 17, 1773. On the 16th of December, there were many meetings between the colonists and the governor with a large meeting being called in the evening. An estimation of over 5,000 people were in attendance. There has always been much conjecture as to the role Samuel Adams might have played in what is now known as the Boston Tea Party. What we do know is that Samuel Adams ended this meeting with the statement, "This meeting can do nothing more to save the country."

At the Boston Harbor, shortly after Adams had spoken what some people believe was a signal, a group of men disguised as Indians, bordered three ships in the harbor with tea as a part of their cargo, and threw all the tea aboard the three ships into the water. No damage was done to the ships or other cargo on the ships.

Of course, the King was livid when he heard what had been done. On May 10, of 1774, word came from London that the Port Bill would be imposed on Boston. This act would place a blockade on Boston. As of June 1, 1774, no ship would be allowed to enter or leave the port until Massachusetts had paid in full the loss inflicted on the evening of December 16, 1773.

The Port Act was just the first in a series of Acts imposed by Parliament that became known as the Coercive Acts or the Intolerable Acts. To follow was the Massachusetts Government Act, which restricted Massachusetts self-governing, by eliminating all democratic held town meetings and required the governor's council be an appointed body and not an elected body as it had always been.

The Administration of Justice Act followed. This act made all British officials immune from criminal prosecution in Massachusetts, but instead, at the request of the British officials, they could be tried in another colony or even in London. The Quartering Act quickly followed. This act required colonists to house and quarter British troops on demand, including in their private homes as a last resort, and receive in compensation what the British government determined they would pay.

More important than the acts themselves was the response of the other colonies to these Acts. Parliament and the King hoped that the acts would separate Boston and New England from the rest of the colonies and prevent unified resistance to British rule. They expected the rest of the colonies would abandon Bostonians to British martial law. Instead, the other colonies rushed to Boston's defense, sending supplies, and forming their own Provincial Congresses to discuss British misrule and mobilize resistance to the crown. Much of this came about because of the communication system that had already been established due to the prior efforts of Samuel Adams.

It was determined that it would be in the best interest of all the colonies to hold a congress to discuss the possibility of a unified response to the

King and Parliament. In September 1774, the First Continental Congress met in Philadelphia and began orchestrating that united resistance to British rule in America. Samuel Adams was one of the Representatives, representing Massachusetts. This was the first time Samuel Adams had ever been outside Massachusetts.

The Massachusetts delegation was held in awe and in fear by the other delegations from the other colonies. The name Samuel Adams was a name the delegates from the other colonies had heard for many years. As might be expected, many had prejudged him. Samuel Adams was aware of his reputation and knew he and the Massachusetts delegation as a whole would be viewed as rebels, especially by the many delegates who preferred the colonists remain as subjects to the King, but have the terms of their charters upheld.

Even so, on October 20, 1774, the First Continental Congress adopted the Articles of Association, which stated that if the Intolerable Acts were not repealed by December 1, 1774, a boycott of British goods would begin in all the colonies. The repeal of the Intolerable acts meant that Massachusetts would not be liable for the payment of the tea destroyed during the Boston Tea Party, and the Boston Harbor Blockade would be lifted immediately.

The Articles also outlined plans for an embargo on exports if the Intolerable Acts were not repealed before September 10, 1775. Lastly and very importantly, even though not expecting the standoff in Massachusetts would explode into full-scale war, the First Continental Congress agreed to reconvene in Philadelphia on May 10, 1775, which it did. It became known as the Second Continental Congress. It was at this Congress the Declaration of Independence was drafted and adopted.

Joseph Galloway, a moderate Representative from Pennsylvania, and not a fan of Samuel Adams, observed what had happened in the First Continental Congress and why Samuel Adams came to be seen as the person who steered America toward independence. Galloway saw Samuel Adams as "a man who though by no means remarkable for brilliant abilities, yet is equal to most men in popular intrigue, and the management of a faction." In short, Samuel Adams had the skills of a master politician. In addition, Galloway joined many others who expressed amazement at his energy and dedication. Galloway observed that Adams, "eats little, drinks little, sleeps little, thinks much, and is most decisive and indefatigable in the pursuit of his objects." Having lost more than one tussle with Adams, Galloway came away transfixed by what he considered Adam's evil political genius. "It was the man," Galloway opined, "who by his superior application managed at once the faction in Congress at Philadelphia, and the factions in New England." (1)

In April of 1775, the Revolutionary War began when the British army marched out of Boston and clashed with colonists at the Battles of Lexington and Concord. The British set out to destroy weapons the colonists had gathered and to arrest Samuel Adams and John Hancock. Adams and Hancock escaped from Lexington thanks to being warned by Paul Revere on his famous ride to warn that the "British are coming".

In 1776, Samuel Adams signed the Declaration of Independence, a document that declared:

The unanimous Declaration of the thirteen united States of America, When in the Course of human events, it becomes necessary for one people to dissolve the political bands which have connected them with another, and to assume among the powers of the earth, the separate and equal station to which the Laws of Nature and of Nature's God entitle them, a decent respect to the opinions of mankind requires that they should declare the causes which impel them to the separation.

Samuel Adams' most important contribution to America's cause, however, was that, in his distant cousin John Adams' words, he had "the most thorough understanding of liberty," the central spark in America's creation.

With liberty far less understood and defended today, the insights of Samuel Adams, the Father of the Revolution deserve remembering:

1. Among the natural rights of the colonists are these: first, a right to life; secondly, to liberty; thirdly to property; together with the right to support and defend them.

2. The natural liberty of man is not to be under the will or legislative authority of man.

3. Every man has an equal right by honest means to acquire property, and pursue his own happiness, and none can consistently control or interrupt him in the pursuit unalienable rights are held sacred.

4. The right to freedom being the gift of Almighty God, it is not in the power of man to alienate this gift.

5. Our unalterable resolution would be to be free.

6. Without liberty and equality [under the law], there cannot exist the assurance of this to every citizen, that his own personal safety and rights are secure the end and design of all free and lawful governments.

7. It is the greatest absurdity to suppose it in the power of one, or any number of men, at the entering into society, to renounce their essential rights, or the means of preserving those rights.

8. All might be free if they valued freedom, and valued it as they should.

9. Our contest is whether there shall be left to mankind an asylum on earth for civil and religious liberty.

10. The most glorious legacy we can bequeath to posterity is liberty the only true security is liberty!

11. While the people are virtuous, they cannot be subdued; but once they lose their virtue, they will be ready to surrender their liberties.

12. While a people retain a just sense of Liberty the insolence of power will forever be despised.

13. There is a degree of watchfulness over all men possessed of power upon which the liberties of mankind must depend. It is necessary to guard against the infirmities of the best as well as the wickedness of the worst.

14. Let us contemplate our forefathers, and posterity, and resolve to maintain the rights bequeathed to us from the former for the sake of the latter.

15. It is a tremendously important and never-ending problem for the self-governing American people to be ever alert and vigorously active in

combating wherever necessary, any and all threats to Individual liberty and to its supporting system of constitutionally limited government.

16. The liberties of our country, the freedom of our civil constitution, are worth defending at all hazards; and it is our duty to defend them against all attacks.

17. It is now high time for the people of this country to explicitly declare whether they will be free men or slaves.

18. If ye love the tranquility of servitude better than the animating contest of freedom may posterity forget that you were our countrymen.

"It does not take a majority to prevail but an irate tireless minority keen on setting brushfires of freedom in the minds of men." Samuel Adams

(1)   Chapter 7, Samuel Adams The Life of an American Revolutionary.

9. SETTING BRUSHFIRES OF FREEDOM

**"It does not take a majority to prevail but rather an irate, tireless minority, keen on setting brushfires of freedom in the minds of men."
Samuel Adams**

What is a brushfire of freedom?

Merriam-Webster defines a brushfire as: involving mobilization only on a small and local scale.

Dictionary.com defines brushfire as: limited in scope, area, or importance, as some labor disputes or local skirmishes.

Urban dictionary defines brushfire as: when information, often gossip, travels quickly and exponentially from person to person via text or social media often times spreading far beyond the initial intended audience.

When we use the definition from these sources, we can see that to set a brushfire is not to engage a nation, a state, or even a city on our own. If the brushfire spreads, it will be because of what I will refer to as the multiplier effect, or when I engage one person, they engage two more, who engage two more and on and on. The people to whom we speak are those close to us such as family, friends, and acquaintances. Very seldom would we set a brushfire through a complete stranger; however, it is not out of the question. It could be that person sitting in the seat next to us on an airplane.

Rumors or gossip are associated with brushfires far more than would meaningful topics such as freedom, liberty, property, republic, or the meaning of the United States Constitution. We have probably all played the game where a person whispers something into the ear of another and so on and so on. Inevitably when the statement is returned to the person who started the game, they are hearing something completely different from what they initially stated.

Another example of this type of brushfire would be the spreading of gossip as in, "Girl, when I told Cindy that Mavis was breaking up with Carl she got right on her phone and started a brushfire. It was not but 10 minutes before someone calls to tell me like I was not the one to break that story but now Mavis is mad because George heard from Alyssa and told Carl. I need to learn to keep my mouth shut."

These are, of course, not what we want to accomplish when we attempt to set a brushfire of freedom. It should be our goal to be clear and precise in what we communicate, so the recipient can ponder the idea. Initially, we would not expect the recipient to spread the idea or thought. Remember, the individual does not necessarily agree with what we have communicated. If they did agree, we would be simply, as the saying goes, "singing to the choir." This is not necessarily a bad thing, because many times the members of the choir need to clarify and be reinforced, but that is not what would necessarily fall into the category of setting a brushfire of freedom. When Samuel Adams introduced this concept, he meant to set that brushfire with somebody who opposed his viewpoint, or was neutral.

In studying Samuel Adams approach, which was amazingly effective, we must understand that to be effective, you cannot be dogmatic, you cannot argue, and even debating is not a good idea. The initial goal is not even necessarily to persuade. The initial goal is to raise a question in the other persons mind about why they believe what they believe. In the case of Samuel Adams, he would have wanted to raise a question in a Tories mind by asking under what authority the Tory believes Parliament had a right to tax a people who had no representation in Parliament. Or when the British troops were occupying Boston prior to the Boston Massacre, Samuel Adams might have asked a Tory why a Parliament and King, who said they wanted harmonious relationships with the people of Boston, would place British troops in Boston for the purpose of controlling and directing the activities of the people against their will, soldiers the people viewed not as just a nuisance, but a threat.

The communications psychologist John Marshall Roberts said that there are three ways of converting people to a cause: by threat of force, by intellectual argument, and by inspiration.

The most effective of these methods, Roberts said, is aligning communication about your cause with the most deeply held values and aspirations of your friends, relatives, neighbors, and fellow citizens. To get people's total, lasting, and unwavering support, in other words, we should try neither to cajole them judgmentally, nor convince them forcefully. We should inspire them toward a vision that they—not we—can really care about.

In order to do this, we have to understand what they believe, not what we think they believe. We can do this if we ask them questions such as, would you rephrase that so I can understand it better; what does that really mean, or we ask them if what they are really saying is, and then we rephrase the question. When doing this, I am not challenging their belief, but trying to understand them better. What we know is we cannot convince anybody to change their mind, they must decide to change their mind themselves. The more they talk, the more we learn that enables us to ask better questions. Our goal at this point is to have them start to question their beliefs and to have them start to suspect that perhaps there are some problems with their belief system. We know a brushfire of freedom has been set when they start to ask us questions about how our ideas differ from theirs and why what we believe is better. Even at this time, it is best if we can lead them to the point where they say that perhaps our way might work.

This process could, and most often will, transpire over a period of time.

Per Roberts, to inspire another to change their minds is the best way. If we use force, be it physical or mental force, we ultimately drive the other individual into their belief system deeper than before. We have not in any way set a brushfire of freedom. To try to persuade with facts, is just another form of mental force. The collectivist holds their beliefs, not because of facts or results, but because of ideology. If I give them a fact, they rebut with a different fact or argument, and then within a short period of time that is where the conversation has gone, to an argument. A collectivist can only be persuaded when they see the error of their way, and so our job is to lead them to the light.

In "The Art of War," Sun Tzu said, "Know the enemy and know yourself; in a hundred battles you will never be in peril. When you are ignorant of the enemy, but know yourself, your chances of winning or losing are equal. If ignorant both of your enemy and yourself, you are certain in every battle to be in peril."

In preparing to become a member of the irate, tireless, minority keen on setting brushfires of freedom, we must come to know ourselves. We must know and understand why we believe what we believe. We must study and understand what freedom and liberty mean. We must study and understand why, in a free society based on individualism, we not only believe, but practice completely what we are told in the Declaration of Independence, "we are endowed by our Creator with certain unalienable rights." We must completely understand why our founders established a Republic and not a democracy. We must understand completely why the principles of "rule of law" and "rights of the minority" are so critical to our freedom.

In the book "The Road to Tyranny", I discuss the principles upon which our nation was founded and go into detail on why those principles are so critical to maintaining a free society. I discuss the differences between individualism and collectivism. The differences are so critical to understand because they are the differences that determine if a people are living in a free society or if the people are slaves to the state.

I also expend on the principles so critical to a society based on the concept of individualism. These principles would be rule of law, limited government, divided government, and sovereignty of the people. As adherence to these principles fluctuates, so does the freedom and liberty of the people. All of these principles are equally important to maintaining a free society. The importance of each of these principles is a predominant part of our Constitution. All of these principles were debated thoroughly at the Constitutional Convention. It is important we know and understand what they are and why our founders believed they were so critical to our long-term freedom that each became a fundamental element of the Constitution.

Never forget, our nation is unique. We are the first nation, and I would argue the only nation, founded on the critical foundation of natural rights. It is so important to us as members of the minority keen on setting those brushfires of freedom, that we understand why a foundation of natural rights is paramount to our freedom and liberty. You must understand not only that there is a difference between a natural right and an entitlement, but also what that difference is and why it is so important. I discuss this in my book "Two Visions of America".

In "Two Visions of America" you will also learn what rights are discussed in the Declaration of Independence, the United States Constitution, and The Bill of Rights. You will learn why the Bill of Rights was added to the United States Constitution and why these specific amendments were included. Thomas Jefferson said the tenth amendment is the very foundation of the Constitution. Many people will quote the tenth amendment but ignore the ninth amendment. Both are equally important. The tenth talks about the limitations placed on the power of the federal government while the ninth talks about the unlimited liberties protected by the Constitution for the people.

Do not become daunted. Based on the knowledge many already have, a review, even a read of "The Road to Tyranny" and "Two Visions of America" and you will have a working foundation necessary to be an effective brushfire setter.

Sun Tzu also said you must know your enemy. You cannot be dismissive of the enemy. It is as critical to know who your enemy is as to know your enemy. Over the years, it was simple to know who your enemy was. They were the people over the hill, across the river, or charging at us on the steppe. The enemy was identified because they wore different uniforms and had different colored vehicles.

When Sun Tzu said you must know your enemy, he meant that you must not only be able to identify your enemy based on physical or visual characteristics, he also meant you must understand the tendencies of your enemy, you must understand how your enemy thinks, you must know your enemy so well that you understand what they will do or say before they do or say. And yes, you must understand that your enemy is living among us; they could be our acquaintances, our friends, and even our family members. We do not identify them based on physical or visual attributes, but we identify them based on their ideological beliefs.

Samuel Adams told us, "The liberties of our country, the freedom of our civil constitution, are worth defending against all hazards: And it is our duty to defend them against all attacks."

Our enemy would be those who are a hazard to the liberties of our country, the freedom of our civil constitution. Our enemy would be those who wish to control and or eliminate our natural rights, those who wish to destroy our Republic, those who wish to abolish rule of law, limited government, divided government, and wish for government to be the sovereign and the people to be slaves to the state. Our enemy would be those who believe our Constitution is an outdated document and the liberties it protects should no longer be protected. Our enemy would be those who no longer cherish and protect our heritage.

The enemy of individualism or the American way, are the collectivists. I have discussed collectivists before. Collectivism is an all-encompassing term that includes the isms, such as Marxism, communism, socialism, progressives, and today's Democrat party. A basic definition of a collectivist is relating to those who practice the principle of giving a group priority over each individual in it. Collectivism requires such things as conformity in thought, accepted limitations on individuals imposed by the group, belief in and desire for economic equality, demonization and elimination of all who seek to achieve and excel, to have all life, liberty, and property be controlled by and granted by the dictates of the collective, and adherence to Marx's command for distribution; "from each according to their ability to each according to their needs."

If we study the collectivists over the years, we learn that they have many common traits. It is as if they have common DNA traits just as family members would have. If we would examine what some of those common DNA traits are, we could have a much better idea who the enemy is, that enemy of what we would commonly call the American way. Here are some of those DNA traits.

The collectivist would have no standard if it were not for a double standard. They truly operate by the axiom of "do what I say and not what I do." Karl Marx clearly demonstrates this double standard principle. Let me use two specific illustrations.

Marx, in the Communist Manifesto stated, as you will remember, that there should be no right to inheritance, but 100% of an estate should be returned to the state or collective. When Jenny Marx's mother died, remember, Karl and Jenny kept 100% of what they received and gave nothing to anybody else including the collective or the state. When Karl Marx's mother died, they again retained every penny he received and shared nothing with anybody, including the collective or the state.

Throughout their entire careers, Karl Marx and Friedrich Engels damned the evils of capitalism and sang the praises of socialism. They stated in the Communist Manifesto that all productive property should be owned and controlled by the collective or the state. They both stated that all should receive based on need and not on individual production.

Friedrich Engels, like Marx, was born into a wealthy family. Engels' father owned textile mills. Friedrich went to work for one of these textile mills in Manchester, England, and became an owner. It was from his abundant earnings that he was able to assist the Marx family.

When Engels retired from his Mill, he sold his ownership share. It enabled him to live a very comfortable life, even after giving Karl and Jenny Marx a substantial annuity so they could live quite comfortably the rest of their lives In addition, Engels was extremely fond of the three Marx girls and gave them substantial initial distributions and then helped them along the way. At his death, the will of Engels revealed he was worth $4 million +, owning shares in several different companies.

This double standard has been common with the collectivist movement. The members of the ruling party live comfortable and financially carefree lives, having special access to the finest in luxury, while the people live in poverty, many times starving.

This double standard extends to all areas of life. We hear conservative news outlets continuously refer to the double standards of the left in cases of finances, morality, sexuality, and so many areas. The standard the collectivist applies diligently against an individualist is completely reversed when under similar circumstances the violating individual is a collectivist. This is their DNA; if it were not for double standards, they would have no standards.

The collectivist lives by the axiom, "the ends always justify the means."

Lenin explained, "There are no morals in politics; there is only experience. A scoundrel may be of use because he is a scoundrel"

Lenin went on to explain, "The revolutionary who pauses before the sanctity of the law in the moment of heated battle is no good. If the law obstructs the progress of the revolution, it should be overturned or amended. All means are good in the fight for power."

Lenin continued, "We respect everything that is done in the interests of the cause of the proletariat. Is there such a thing as Communist morality? Are there Communist ethics? Of course, there are! But our morality is entirely dependent upon the interests of the proletariat in its class war. We say: morality is what serves to destroy the old society. And the dictatorship of the proletariat means precisely totally unrestricted power, unconstrained by any laws or any rules at all, and based directly upon force."

And then he stated to what extent you could extend this force, "You can't make a revolution wearing white gloves. Until there is no violence against the masses, there is no other pathway to power. One must promote the energy and mass-character of terror. Mass searches. Execution for holding weapons. Merciless terror against kulaks, priests, and the White Army. You must lock up suspicious characters in concentration camps. You must execute conspirators and anyone who wavers, asking no questions and allowing for no idiotic red tape. You need to make the people see what you are doing and tremble for hundreds of kilometers around. Let 90% of the Russian people perish if it allows just 10% to live to see a worldwide revolution."

Saul Alinsky went on to tell us, "The third rule of ethics of means and ends is that in war the end justifies almost any means."

The collectivist of today follows the dictates of Lenin in that they remove the term "almost" from the statement by Alinsky.

Those who adhere to the traits of double standards and having any means justified by the ends, we can state, are not virtuous people. There are no common rules, standards, or morality that dictate their behavior. This type of behavior is a part of their personal lives and their professional or business lives. When Samuel Adams learned that a former colleague of his, Dr. Church, had sold out his country to the British for monetary gain, Samuel Adams responded that it could not be that much of a surprise since Dr. Church was notorious for cheating on his wife.

We were told continuously by our founding fathers how critical it was that we continued to be a virtuous people and elect virtuous people to be our representatives. Samuel Adams, being an exemplary husband and father as well as an individual of unquestioned integrity, and morality, told us of the importance of virtue, along with natural rights and liberties, in maintaining our Republic and passing it on to future generations.

"A general dissolution of the principles and manners will more surely overthrow the liberties of America than the whole force of the common enemy. While the people are virtuous, they cannot be subdued; but once they lose their virtue, they will be ready to surrender their liberties to the first external or internal invader. If virtue and knowledge are diffused among the people, they will never be enslaved. This will be their great security." Samuel Adams

"No people will tamely surrender their Liberties, nor can any be easily subdued, when knowledge is diffused, and Virtue is preserved. On the Contrary, when People are universally ignorant, and debauched in their Manners, they will sink under their own weight without the Aid of foreign Invaders." Samuel Adams

The collectivist has always understood the danger that virtue is to their conforming and equal classless society. A virtuous person is a person that will not conform to dictates that are contrary to the moral fiber to which they profess and adhere. We learn that a critical element to virtue in any society is a strong family unit where values are taught and exhibited by parents and not by the state. When the state is the purveyor of values, conformity becomes the rule and virtue is limited if not eliminated. Collectivist aspiring despots always have as one of their immediate goals to destroy the family. Lenin absolutely did as we have discussed.

"Destroy the family, you destroy the country." Vladimir Lenin

Lenin also understood that even discussion of liberties and natural rights could not be tolerated. All rights and liberties were under the control of the state and must remain so.

"Ideological talk and phrase mongering about political liberties should be disposed with; all that is mere chatter and phrase mongering. We should get away from those phrases." Vladimir Lenin

One of these liberties that must be controlled by the state was the health care of the family.

"Socialized medicine is the keystone to the arch of the socialist state." Vladimir Lenin

Another liberty that must be taken from the people was the right to bear arms.

"A system of licensing and registration is the perfect device to deny gun ownership to the bourgeoise." Vladimir Lenin

Along with controlling speech and assembly, Lenin understood that a free press was not tolerable.

"When one makes a Revolution, one cannot mark time; one must always go forward - or go back. He who now talks about the 'freedom of the press' goes backward, and halts our headlong course towards Socialism." Vladimir Lenin

"The press should be not only a collective propagandist and a collective agitator, but also a collective organizer of the masses." Vladimir Lenin

Yes, Lenin clearly understood the danger of liberty and virtue to a socialist society, which he stated is simply the gateway to communism

"It is true that liberty is precious; so precious that it must be carefully rationed." Vladimir Lenin

Our Republic cannot exist, no Republic could exist, with the beliefs and standards of the collectivist (Marxist, communist, socialist, progressive – all virtually the same) ideas and standards. If we are to retain our Republic built on the concept of natural rights, we must fight to save it, we must start to set brushfires of freedom in the minds of people. I will repeat that to do this we must understand ourselves, our beliefs, the collectivist, and the collectivist beliefs.

Samuel Adams did not try to set brushfires of freedom in the minds of the hard and fast loyalists to the British crown, people like Governor's Hutchinson or Gage for instance. It also would have been a waste of time and effort to try to set brushfires of freedom in the minds of Marx, Engels, or Lenin.

Samuel Adams did concentrate his efforts to set brushfires of freedom in the minds of those who were what we might term, "fence sitters." That would be those who might be leaning toward the British, but were not sure why, those who would bend with the current or convenient thought of the day, those who claimed to be Whigs, which was the party of Adams, but were hot and cold, and those who avoided the issue by claiming they just did not understand or could not be bothered.

It is these groups that could have some of the characteristics of the collectivist, but probably not all. It is also these groups that probably recognize these DNA characteristics of the collectivist, but do not identify with them and probably recognize them for the evil they are. It is the people who might identity as progressive or liberal, but still stand for the National Anthem and the Pledge of Allegiance for instance. They do not understand the differences between natural rights and an entitlement, or a Republic and a democracy, but still salute the American flag. It is these people who will claim on the one hand they are being loyal to a particular political party because their parents were and they have always been, even though they disagree, and their parents would have disagreed with all of the party's current platform planks. It is that person who says they could never vote for the other party because the other party has no compassion, or whatever, but nevertheless agrees with the platform planks of the party.

We all know these people. When we engage these people with facts and evidence, we become frustrated because they will refute the fact or use a bumper sticker or 30 second sound bite to refute, and the conversation ends in at best a debate, but more often an argument. You cannot change them; they must change themselves. All you can do is set a brushfire of freedom in their mind. All you can do is plant a seed. **HOW????**

10. HOW????

This is the critical question; how to set that brushfire of freedom. All of us have heard the comment that I really told so and so what is right, or I buried him with facts, or he now knows just how dumb he is and will never give me that nonsense again. We might have impressed ourselves or another who agrees with us, but we lost the individual we might have had a chance to convince prior to our **TELLING THEM.**

Remember how we learned earlier what is the best way to inspire another to change their mind? If we use force, be it physical, or mental force, we ultimately drive them into their beliefs deeper than before. We have not in any way set a brushfire of freedom. To try to persuade with facts is just another form of mental force. The collectivist holds their beliefs, not because of facts or results, but it is ideological. If I give them a fact, they rebut with a different fact or argument and then within a short period of time; that is where the conversation has gone, to an argument.

I took these excerpts from an article I read by Ozan Varol, who is a rocket scientist, turned author, and tenured law professor at Lewis & Clark Law School. He is a law professor; yes, he is a leftist, but what he had to say in "Facts don't change people's minds, here is what does," was spot on, so I will share it.

"If you had asked me this question—How do you change a mind? —two years ago, I would have given you a different answer.

As a former scientist, I would have cautioned you to rely on objective facts and statistics. Develop a strong case for your side, back it up with hard, cold, irrefutable data, and voila!

Drowning the other person with facts, I assumed, was the best way to prove that global warming is real, the war on drugs has failed, or the current business strategy adopted by your risk-averse boss with zero imagination is not working.

Since then, I have discovered a significant problem with this approach.

It does not work.

The mind does not follow the facts. Facts, as John Adams put it, are stubborn things, but our minds are even more stubborn. Doubt is not always resolved in the face of facts for even the most enlightened among us, however credible and convincing those facts might be.

As a result of the well-documented confirmation bias, we tend to undervalue evidence that contradicts our beliefs and overvalue evidence that confirms them. We filter out inconvenient truths and arguments on the opposing side. As a result, our opinions solidify, and it becomes increasingly harder to disrupt established patterns of thinking.

If facts do not work, how do you change a mind— whether it is your own or your neighbor's?

Give the mind an out.

We are reluctant to acknowledge mistakes. To avoid admitting we were wrong, we will twist ourselves into positions that even seasoned yogis cannot hold.

The key is to trick the mind by giving it an excuse. Convince your own mind (or your friend) that your prior decision or prior belief was the right one given what you knew, but now that the underlying facts have changed, so should the mind.

But instead of giving the mind an out, we often go for a punch to the gut. We belittle the other person ("I told you so"). We ostracize ("Basket of deplorables"). We ridicule ("What an idiot").

Schadenfreude (pleasure derived by someone from another person's misfortune) might be your favorite pastime, but it has the counterproductive effect of activating the other person's defenses and solidifying their positions. The moment you belittle the mind for believing in something, you have lost the battle. At that point, the mind will dig in rather than give in. Once you have equated someone's beliefs with ideocracy, changing that person's mind will require nothing short of an admission that they are unintelligent. And that is an admission that most minds are not willing to make.

"The moment you belittle the mind for believing in something, you've lost the battle."

"When your beliefs are entwined with your identity, changing your mind means changing your identity. That's a really hard sell."

Humans operate on different frequencies. If someone disagrees with you, it is not because they are wrong, and you are right. It is because they believe something that you do not believe.

The challenge is to figure out what that thing is and adjust your frequency."

End of excerpts from Ozan Varol. Highlights and comment defining Schadenfreude are mine.

We cannot change another person's mind for them. We cannot sell somebody something they do not want. We can plant a seed, water it, tend it, and hopefully harvest it. Maybe we will be the planter, the waterer, the tenderer, or the harvester, but very seldom will we play all the roles. The other person must decide they came to a new understanding, be able to rationalize that what they now believe is what they have always believed but something has changed so they must also, or that they want what you are offering. The other person is typically the harvester because they come to the new conclusion on their own. This is when the new idea is most solidly set in their minds. This is the best outcome and it is the outcome that leads the other person to become part of the minority that is keen on setting brushfires of freedom.

It cannot be emphasized strongly enough that we cannot change another person's mind, they must change it. In order to do this, we must not challenge their belief as being necessarily wrong, but lead them down the path of questioning if their belief is correct, or even if there is perhaps a better way. If we can ask the proper questions or lead them to the point where they ask themselves the proper question, we have at least begun the process of setting that brushfire.

Of course, prior to this point, we have taken the time to learn who we are, what we believe, and why we believe what we do believe. We do not yet know if the other person knows what they believe and why they believe it. If we have done our proper preparation, we do know what the collectivist believes and why they believe what they believe. It is important we understand if the other person is a bumper sticker and 30 second sound bite collectivist, or if they have a good grasp as to why they are collectivists. We can only learn this by listening and asking questions. Remember, we know what we know, but we do not know what they know. If we are trying to learn and understand, we do not achieve this by talking, but by listening. It is always easier to make a sale when the prospect tells us what they want, and how we should sell them. That is why we brushfire setters must become great listeners. Listen to learn and not for the purpose of being able to set the stage to tell the other person what we think and why they are wrong.

Many years ago, I was fortunate to take a class put on by the "Sandler Sales Institute." The premise of the sales course was that you must learn from the client what you need to do in order to have him purchase the product you had. You could not do this if you were busy telling him about all the special features and benefits your product had. You could only accomplish your purpose if you were able to lead the client to the point where they would ask you if you could help them solve the problem that person had told you they had. You must lead that person to arrive at the conclusion that what you had was in their best interest.

People, salespeople, and others talk far more than they listen, and typically their favorite subject is themself. A good setter of brushfires of freedom must learn that this is not about them but about the other person. If the setter of brushfires of freedom finds they are talking more than 30% of the time, they are driving the other person toward collectivism and away from freedom.

One of the methods used by the "Sandler Sales System" to keep the conversation headed in the proper direction is called "reversing." It is critical that when you employ this method you do it honestly, that is that you are genuinely interested in what the other person has to say. For instance, if the collectivist says that they believe compassion to another is the best method of helping them and their party is a party of compassion, rather than telling them they are dead wrong because socialism always has a higher rate of poverty than capitalism does (which is true) and starting an argument, a better response would be to simply say "that is interesting, but tell me what does compassion mean to you." There is no right or wrong answer to that question because only the other person knows what compassion means to them. But their answer good give you an excellent idea as to whether or not they are bumper sticker and 30 second sound bite collectivists, or if they have a more deeply formed opinion and reason for holding this viewpoint.

The Sandler method explains that by "reversing" a question, I have the other person talking again, shifted the focus to them, and flattered the other person by showing a genuine interest in what they think. I could also have helped the other person arrive at a better idea of what they do mean by compassion, because for many people it helps them to understand their thoughts better when they verbalize. It also gives me information, gives me more credibility because I did not argue or attack, and most importantly, I will have learned something about them.

Another method of accomplishing much of the above, but important because you are using a different approach, is the method called "Testing the Water." In our example about compassion, the "Testing the Water" approach could be something like, "I get the feeling that you believe compassion is extremely critical, is that a fair statement, and if so why." Rather than "reversing" on the next topic, you would probably want to use the "Test the Water" approach so your approach does not become redundant.

When you perceive the conversation is taking a direction that might be leading toward debating statistics, or becoming an argument, a great approach is to step back a minute and say something like, "If you had a magic wand and could create the perfect society, what would that society be." When we can have the other person speak in ideals, this will also give us an excellent idea as to what they genuinely believe and where I might be able to set a solid brushfire of freedom. For instance, they might say that in the ideal society there would be no need for compassion because all would be able to pursue and attain their own wants and needs.

The approach would then be to reverse wants and needs by asking them to define wants and needs. You would then simply reply with something like "what a wonderful society. You have given me some real food for thought, I know I am going to study which approach, capitalism, or socialism, has come closest to achieving that goal. Does that sound like a worthwhile undertaking for you as well?"

The brushfire of freedom, in this instance would be, that capitalism has throughout history always had less poverty, more opportunity, and a much higher standard of living. If the collectivist will research the question openly and honestly, the only honest conclusion they could reach is that capitalism is a far more compassionate system if we define compassion to mean less poverty.

Some other examples would be:

The rich need to pay their fair share.

Interesting, and what do you think their fair share would be?

Interesting, you say that. We could look at it this way and say that all income really belongs to the government and then the government would tell us what we should have, or we could look at it from the standpoint that the income is really the individuals and then each individual determines what they should pay.

What do you think would be the best way?

Under which system do you think people would be most productive? Why?

Is it important that the people in the society are productive? Why?

College is a basic right and should be free.

Do you think than that all people should go to college?

What about those people who do not go to college, should they be taxed to pay for those who do and if so, is that fair?

Supposedly those that go to college have an opportunity to make far more than those that do not. Should the college people than split their income with those who paid for their education?

How do you make this system fair?

We should not have borders.

Do you mean that anybody and everybody can come into your country anytime?

If that happens, do you have a country?

Do you have citizenship?

How do you know who is here and how do you collect taxes from them, or not?

Do you have requirements for drivers' licenses, for car insurance, how do you identify anybody if there has been no registration?

How do your schools' function with kids coming and going?

How do banks make loans when they have no idea to whom they are lending money?

How do you ever have elections when you have no idea if the person is a citizen or not?

How do you have a country?

People believe what they believe for many different reasons. Many people have no idea why they believe what they believe. Many people have never been asked to share or explain their beliefs. It has been my experience that the more I can get a bumper sticker and 30 second sound bite collectivist to verbalize their beliefs, the deeper is the brushfire of freedom set. We never want to say, see I told you so, or I knew you were dead wrong. However, they rationalize their belief system is simply fine, so long as the brushfire of freedom is set and begins to burn deeply within them. Hopefully, they will become a part of the minority setting brushfires of freedom in the minds of others.

This is not about you or me being right or correct. This is about you and me understanding that our freedom and liberty can only be saved and restored as we follow in the footsteps of the Father of the Revolution, Samuel Adams, and make it our purpose and goal to set brushfires of freedom in the minds of others.

BIBLIOGRAPHY

Alexander, John K., "Samuel Adams, The Life of an American Revolutionary" Lanham, Maryland, Rowman & Littlefield Publishers, Inc., 2011

Brown, Archie, "The Rise and Fall of Communism" New York, New York, HarperCollins Publishers, 2009

Edwards, Paul, General Editor, "Marx Selections" New York, New York, Macmillan Publishers Company, 1988

Ferguson, Robert A., Introduction and Notes, "The Federalist" New York, New York, Barnes & Noble Books, 2006

Gellately, Robert, "Lenin, Stalin, and Hitler" New York, New York, Vintage Books A Division of Random House, Inc., 2008

Irvin, Benjamin H., "Samuel Adams Son of Liberty, Father of Revolution" Oxford, New York, Oxford University Press, 2002

Leatherbarrow, William, and Offord, Derek, Edited by, "A History of Russian Thought" New York, New York, Cambridge University Press, 2010

Locke, John, "Two Treatises of Government" Edited by Mark Goldie, London, England, Orion Publishing Group, 1993

Puls, Mark, "Samuel Adams Father of the American Revolution" New York, New York, Palgrave Macmillan, 2006

Rappaport, Helen, "Caught in the Revolution" New York, New York, St Martin's Press, 2016

Read, Christopher, "Lenin" New York, New York, Routledge, 2005

Sandler, David, H., "You Can't Teach a Kid to Ride a Bike at a Seminar" United States of America, Bay Head Publishing, Inc., 1995

Service, Robert, "Lenin A Biography" London, England, Pan Books, 2002

Tucker, Robert C., Edited by "The Marx-Engels Reader" Second Edition, New York, New York, W.W. Norton & Company, Inc., 1978

West, Thomas G., "The Political Theory of the American Founding Natural Rights Policy, and the Moral Conditions of Freedom" New York, New York, Cambridge University Press 2017

About the Author

Don Jans is a student of history. This study has taken him into the study of Marxism. In addition to reading, he has extended his studies through travel and has been able to go to many different countries and not just see historical sites, but learn from those who have studied the different periods and occurrences. Don has taken a particular interest in the Marxist movement and so he has made a point of traveling to many different countries that had been under Communist rule. A part of those travels always includes seeking out those who lived under Communist dictators, or their children. The common comment from these people is how lucky we are in America, and how they wish they could live in such a free nation. Don does not have the heart to explain to them that in America there are many who have as their goal to transform the United States into a nation like the one in which they or their parents lived.

Don is also a speaker and is available to talk to groups throughout the United States. Contact info mygrandchildrensamerica@gmail.com.

Website www.mygrandchildrensamerica.com